My Father's Genes

A Struggle of Self
and a
Willing Spirit

Pat Clark

ISBN: 9781914173073

You can contact Pat Clark at:
pat@opengates.scot

All Scripture quotations are taken from the New International Version unless otherwise stated. Copyright © 1973, 1978 International Bible Society. Published by Hodder and Stoughton.

Dedication

To my darling family.

You are a joy and a blessing.

Commendation

I have known Pat since the late 1980s when he attended the Prison Fellowship drop-in at Hamiltonhill, Glasgow, on Thursdays. He demonstrated a big compassionate heart for men and women coming out of prison and is an excellent communicator to those in our prisons when he visited as a volunteer. Once a year he was assisted by his son Barclay at the Champions weekend in Kilmarnock prison!

Pat also travelled with me in the USA where he shared his testimony to great effect.

I would commend Pat and this book to your attention.

Colin Cuthbert
Formerly Director of Prison Fellowship
(Retired prison and hospital chaplain)

Contents

Foreword		7
Preface		9
Introduction		11
	Part 1	
Chapter 1	Show a Child the Way	15
Chapter 2	A New House	27
Chapter 3	Glasgow Crime Wave	39
Chapter 4	St Joseph's and 'The Brothers'	45
Chapter 5	Wake Up Call! Borstal and Beyond	65
Chapter 6	I See The Bad Moon A-Rising	77
Chapter 7	Ireland	91
Chapter 8	Bingo and the 'Big Hoos'	105
Chapter 9	The Last Sentence	119
Chapter 10	A Phone Call Leads to Breaking Point	141
	Part 2	
Chapter 11	A Divine Encounter	157
Chapter 12	A Changed Life	173
Chapter 13	The Clark Gable Food Bar	189
Chapter 14	The King's Court	207
Chapter 15	Carstairs	219
Chapter 16	India	227
Chapter 17	Egg on Your Face or a Word from God?	235
Chapter 18	Open Gates 2010: Beginnings	241
Chapter 19	Abraham's Wells	251
Epilogue		265

Foreword

About forty years ago at the close of a crowded and powerful Sunday evening service, my dear friend Pat Clark surrendered his life to Jesus.

This particular service was held in the New Life Church in Drumchapel, a sprawling council estate on the furthest western edge of Glasgow's city boundary. In those distant days Drumchapel was affectionately called, *"the Pondarosa"* after a popular cowboy series on BBC TV. This was a passing nod to Drumchapel unfortunately being the "Wild West" of Glasgow!

At the close of the service the guest speaker, Jim Kincaid, a former Church of Scotland minister from Aberdeen, invited anyone who would like to talk to him to see him after the service.

I watched in wonder as a well-known local character made his way to engage Jim in earnest conversation about eternal issues. After a period of deep discussion, Pat Clark bowed his head and opened his heart to the Lordship of Jesus Christ.

If you are wondering what a genuine born-again Christian looks like, then I encourage you to begin reading this heart-warming story and get to know for yourself my dear friend Pat Clark.

Probably a number of Pat's former youthful acquaintances and colleagues are still to this very day in a state of bewilderment how anyone, but especially their local hero Pat Clark, could be so radically and permanently changed from sinner to saint, and from crime to Christ.

However, if any of them ever get within earshot of Pat they will soon learn of Jesus Christ and perhaps, like Pat, surrender their lives to Christ and become part of that never ending, ever lengthening chain of followers of Jesus Christ the Friend of Sinners.

Pat Clark is an ardent follower of Jesus, filled with the dynamic power and creative energy of the Holy Spirit and overflowing with the joy and love of his Saviour, the Lord Jesus Christ.

Pat's new life is a heavenly gift ever flowing to him from God his Father… Yes, Pat really does have his Father's genes and is daily being pumped full of them! This means that Pat can be an "imitator of God", in loving and sacrificial service to those in need.

"Therefore be imitators of God as dear children. And walk in love, as Christ also has loved us and given Himself for us, an offering and a sacrifice to God for a sweet-smelling aroma." Ephesians 5:1,2

"Behold, what manner of love the Father hath bestowed upon us, that we should be called the sons of God." 1 John 3:1 (KJV)

I congratulate Pat for writing this moving testimony of the goodness and grace of God and I whole-heartedly commend, *My Father's Genes* to a wide readership.

Rev Dr Alex Gillies BA, BD, ThM, ThD
Victory Christian Centre, Govan, Glasgow

Preface

I have often heard the saying that being incarcerated is just like a holiday camp for prisoners. Being in a position to judge I can assure you that this saying could not be further from the truth. Never, in all my years of misdemeanours, have I met anyone who was remotely disappointed on their day of release, not one.

In reality we are all prisoners to dark influences of self, with no metal bars or cells attached, but rather to pride, guilt, anger, revenge, greed, lust, racism, fear, drugs, addiction, self-pity, rejection, shame and even condemnation of the past to name but a few.

With each individual dark power being an overlord of the heart, which is the custodian of our peace, they often attack in multiples against the soul of man with no mercy. They work through the mind (fanatic in the attic) as they systematically use the only system they can operate in to get to their destinations of Doubt, Deception, Division and Death.

At the start of a prison sentence you want to find out your liberation date as you buckle down to serve the length of time given. Fulfilling the sentence releases you back to where you came from with an exhaling sigh of relief, but as for self, you are still held prisoner to the inner promptings and powers of the heart.

But there is a release date made for each and every one of us, and that release clause was carried out at Calvary. Jesus cried out *"Tetelestai"* (It is Finished), which was a cry reserved for conquering kings when they returned home victorious with the spoils of a defeated enemy.

Thirty seven years ago I was released eternally when I repented to most of the things mentioned above, when I accepted His Word of *"Tetelestai."*

Yes, I fall daily but by His strength and grace, I get up and start afresh each day in faith. Now, I have a release date from self, a date that only He knows.

I'm no longer a slave to fear for I am a child of God.

Pat

Introduction

Sticks and Stones

How can I grab your attention and keep your interest in the story I am about to tell? If I inform you that God is the main character then that may jettison fifty percent of those mildly interested, but if I tell you that the story to follow is sometimes even stranger than fiction, and true, then I just might be able to hold on to you that little bit longer, maybe longer than could be expected.

Can I first of all say that there is not a person on the planet that does not have something to say about their lives: so each of us has a potential book to write, or at least a story to tell. We are so individually different, so unique and so wonderfully made that it makes me wonder how on earth the masses can be entertained by the modern day theory of evolution that states we came from a puddle of glabber.

Well hopefully these pages can encourage you and enlighten you to see that you are special, and, that you are cared for by the Living God. Make no mistake about this book, it is not about me, it's about what God *was* doing and *is* doing in me. It's all about His protection, His forgiveness, His favour, His direction and His will. So in no way, shape or form would I want to put myself forward as the main subject of this autobiography.

Now that my wee preach is over let me continue…

My tale starts at the first memories I have as a child. My mother was always amazed that I could tell her things that she thought I could not possibly know or remember.

There are six instances I will recount and the reason I do this is to confirm that the God who had His hand on me as a child is the same God that is with me now as an adult. He always was a major part of my life (although my actions did not show it) until I became thirty three. Since then He *is* the major part of my life.

I hope you enjoy the story.

Pat

PART 1

When I am weak He is strong.

2 Corinthians 2:1

1

Show a Child the Way
1949-54

Joy, protection, fear, healing, compassion and work ethics – all from the Gorbals

The six stories I am about to tell might give you an insight as to how I was introduced to joy, protection, fear, compassion, healing and a work ethic.

I know most people would agree that our children are moulded and shaped at an early age. I think the question needs to be asked, how early and for how long, are they moulded till they go on to do their own thing?

Joy – mouse in the bottle

My family of five lived at the corner of Cumberland Street and Thistle Street in a top floor single room that had a nearly clean toilet on the landing. Well, it always looked clean to me on the occasions I saw inside it, probably because I was so young and still in nappies.

There were less than three years between me and my two baby sisters Helen and Sadie. Sadie was a brand new baby and she was demoted to a small cot at the side of the large recess bed while Helen and I slept with our parents.

I remember the morning well as my mother sang her songs while she cleaned the washing in the sink with her scrubbing board using the big block of sunlight soap. All the clothes were rinsed and folded ready for taking into the back court to be hung out to dry.

As the sun shone through the only window of our one room home, my mother reached up to the cupboard and brought out a milk bottle to wash (aye, we washed out the milk bottles in those days).

The scream she let out will remain with me all of my days. She dropped the bottle onto the sink, and shuffled backwards with both feet going like pistons in reverse. With her hands clasped firmly on her chest, and in between the continuous scream, I could hear her call, "Jesus, Mary and Joseph, oh, Jesus Mary and Joseph."

I then heard my father John shouting above the commotion as he sat reading his paper, "For goodness sake Betty, it's only a mouse."

This trivial revelation did not do anything for my mother but my Da thought it was funny. I remember understanding that a mouse had fallen into the bottle and died and this was the cause for my Ma to portray to every neighbour within earshot that she had just witnessed a national disaster.

I do not know how long I laughed with my Da but it seemed forever. I do not know if my two younger sisters were old enough to join in but it was a time of joy (even if it was just between me and my Da, at my Ma's expense) that I can still reflect on to this day.

At any time of laughter I can go back into that wonderful mode of funny contentment that happened all those years ago.

Protection – falling in the puddle

Another experience happened when my Ma put me out to play with some local children. Once again it was a sunny day but the sun was shining upon a cold frost that covered the back courts of our Gorbals tenement.

It must have been a secure place for my Ma was always on hand to shout from our top flat window if I wandered. I think the security I felt might have stemmed from the fact I was dressed up like an Egyptian Mummy.

Being winter, my Ma (like most mothers of that time) had me well and truly wrapped up against the winter cold. A big woolly jumper was the order for the day. On top of the woolly jumper, I was shoe horned into a heavy overcoat which felt so tight. The coat was secured by buttons that strained to hold the garment together. This outer garment was then reinforced by a large scarf that went around the back of my neck before crossing my chest and then going under my arms to meet up at the small of my back on its marathon journey. The scarf was then rewarded with a large silver safety pin that kept me and the clothes all together. My two arms were held firmly in place, straight down, slightly outward, unbendable and unmovable.

The back courts themselves were always dirty with bricks and debris lying around. I must have waddled away from the group of children I had been with, for I found myself at a large puddle that was almost clear of ice. I remember trying to bend down and pick up a piece of the ice at the edge of the puddle. The next thing I realised was that I was falling sidewards and then backwards into the cold stagnant water.

As I lay in the water on my back I opened my eyes and could see the sky through the cold and murky liquid that covered my face by one inch. The puddle itself was not more than twelve inches deep but it was deep enough for my upper torso and head to be submerged.

I could not move but there was a calmness that came over me, the protection I had felt from my clothing was entirely different from the protection I felt from within. I can't remember swallowing any water or struggling to get up (I couldn't if I wanted to anyway with the binding clothes I had on) but what I do remember is the feeling of being safe.

Time seemed to pass without panic before I felt two strong hands gently but firmly get hold of my shoulders from underneath and raise me to my feet (which were still on dry ground) and out of the puddle.

I remember waddling around slowly (thanks to my armour called a coat) looking to see who had assisted me, but saw no one. Whether as a child, and the way I was dressed, there had been someone there or not, I do not know but what I do know is that I was helped from that certain watery grave by hands I did not see.

We have a protector who cares, even when we can't see Him.

Fear – rats in the back

One thing about living in the Gorbals was that the location was shared by an indigenous livestock called "The Backcourt Rat". Now these small animals were not so small if you were a child or a mother who was terrified by a dead mouse in a bottle. But to the rats' credit, they tended to keep to the backcourts and usually worked constant night shift.

On one particular night my Ma was taking me home from visiting a relative. We lived at the corner of the building, which meant that our stairway was nearer the back court than the entrance. In line with the stairway and above our heads was the gas mantle that never seemed to give out enough light, thus flickering shadows played their tricks on scared mothers.

At the back of the close was an open area that took you to the backcourt. It was here that you could make out small darting shadows as they ran past the close's rear opening. You had to look closely at the darker shadows to see the rat run in full flight.

Like Morse Code, there was no uniform to their constant race to and fro, and due to the flickering shadow camouflage from the gas mantle, they blended in perfectly with the darkness. Well, need I say, my Ma only had to be suspicious of any small furry thing darting anywhere to cause her to go into an apocalyptic panic. It was at this point I refused to be held back as a protected child by an over caring scared mother.

I remember so vividly being upset at my Ma's obvious fear (besides I was tired, and fear was not going to stop me getting home), so I pulled on her hand and rushed towards the stairway. With all of my might and with my eyes peeled on the back court I became the barrier that gave her the courage to go the two steps that took us on to the stairway and upwards to safety. Fear was put back to the end of the queue for me.

Healing

Play time on Thistle Street was joy. It was one of the smoothest streets in the Gorbals, with no cobbles or cracks on the perfectly smooth road surface.

The boys had their homemade "boggies" and "girders," while the lassies played with their skipping ropes, their balls against the wall and their "peaver" on the chalked beds expertly drawn on the pavement. In among this eclectic play area was a "fitba" being chased by a dozen "snottery" and unkempt kids.

Oh, I was one of them, and to me at the time it was normality and it was orderly and it was enjoyable.

The "fitba" didn't interfere with the girls banging their tennis balls against the wall as the "boggies" weaved and screeched up the pavements edge making sure they gave the girls who "cawed" their skipping ropes for the wee queue of lassies that was waiting to jump in as one jumped out.

The peaver beds were always being upgraded with a large piece of pipe clay chalk as tiny feet pounded the nine numbers remembering to stay within the perimeter outline. It was at one of these wonderful playtimes that I took ill.

I remember having a cowboy gun and belt on, and I faced a duel to the death with my wee pal who was eyeing me with a determination that I knew I matched. This was serious stuff but as I was about to "draw" I could hear the cacophony of noise that only children can manufacture go quiet, as darkness seemed to wrap itself around me.

The last thing I remember is falling softly to the ground and knowing I was going to be okay.

I don't know how long I was out for but I awoke in the local doctor's surgery with my parents and others looking over me (apparently the football, peaver, ropes and boggies had ceased as my young friends stood outside the surgery waiting to find out about my condition).

I remember my mother's tears and her relief as she gave me a hug that almost knocked me out again. I then heard a voice saying out loud to the crowd (mostly the kids but adults too) in the waiting room that spilled onto the street, "He's okay, he's okay."

It's strange thinking back on this time, but this experience has seen me through a few operations (even a heart bypass) without any fear or animosity. I have always felt that softness of falling and the feeling of security at the time of any health trauma.

After the reassuring hug from my Ma all I could say was "Can ah get a thrupenny bit?" I heard the laughter that ensued but I was disappointed that the money was not forthcoming, even though I had thought that that was the best time to put my case forward for finance.

Compassion

All these memories stem from our tenement "single end" flat, but it was at the same time. Also around this time I was in hospital in a small room that held four grey metal cots. The heavy metal cots had high sides that had to be lifted up before they could come down so to allow a child to be placed or lifted from the cot.

My memory is as clear today as it was then about this incident. I remember it being uncomfortably hot and as I looked up from under my clean hospitalised sheets at the two closed windows high on the wall near the ceiling, I felt a concoction of feelings that centred on abandonment and loneliness and perhaps tinged with a fear of not seeing my parents again.

There were also another two children in the same room with me. I was trying to pluck up the courage to get up and out of the sheets that were tucked in so tightly around me. I must have lain a while when the child across from the foot of my cot whimpered and that gave me a surge and a reason to get up from under the sheets and stand at the bottom of my cot.

I just felt (even as a young child in a cot) that I wanted to help, to be near and to encourage my fellow child inmate that things would be okay (even the concoction of lonely feelings left me while I was doing this).

I got up and as I did, I noticed that the child in the other bed had not moved an inch. I also knew that that child felt the same way as I had. The top of my cot came to under my chin and as I tried to lift it I knew it was too heavy.

I don't know what I said to the hurting child, all I knew was that I had to get out of my prison and be with my hurting friend. So I climbed up and found myself balancing on top of the corner of the cot (that seemed to be built with scaffolding) on my stomach, with one leg on each side of the metal frame.

I then slipped down onto the cool linoleum floor. When I got to the other side of the room my fellow baby inmate was wrapped up like a papoose just as I had been. Tears ran down his/her face (I can't remember if it was a boy or girl) and all I did was put my hand between the bars of the cot and held his/hers.

At that point I felt comforted just as he/she did. Fear left me, as the thought of any consequences of being out of my cot dissolved along with the loneliness of abandonment I had felt.

The reason for this small story is to explain that even as a child, possibly just two or three years old, I felt compassion, even in a small way. Just to add to that thought of compassion and family ethos; I remember so, so clearly when our latest wee sister (Sadie) was a baby, I was three years old and Helen was almost two.

My Ma must have been out, as Helen and I decided to help ourselves to our new baby sibling's bottle of milk. It was probably my idea, but Helen never objected. I "dreeped" over the high recess bed, quickly removed the bottle of white nectar from wee Sadie's possession, before returning to the safety of the bed via a chair, to consume our ill-gotten gain.

Prior to Sadie's arrival and on an earlier occasion I had gone through the same procedure for Helen, but it was not for milk, it was for raw sausage. I can remember the taste to this day. So to say that I had "previous" would be a charge I would plead guilty to.

I was to go on in life to experience a real compassion that showed me how much compassion Father God has for each and every one of us.

Work ethics

The last wee story of this chapter takes me to where my dad earned his living. My wee Da was a hardworking man whose life centred on his young wife and his three young children. He was a great wee guy who loved to make you laugh.

He was totally dedicated to my Ma and all of his family. He was reliable and faithful and I am so proud to have been his son. His life had been lived under a strict father who did not show a father's love to him or his siblings. On this day in particular I was carried (probably by my Ma) into his work. He worked in a shed that "bunched sticks" in the Gorbals area just up from our home.

To explain that, you need to know that in Glasgow there was a big market for fire kindling. This wood kindling was put into bunches and tied, hence "a bunch of sticks." To do this my Da, along with his workmates, sat at two large pieces of wood (logs) cut to size. One was used as the seat and the other was the chopping board. With a sharp metal cleaver they would chop the wood that had been sawn into six inch lengths.

Once they had a pile of these thinly chopped sticks they would lift them and pile them on to their work benches where a metal vice was connected to the edge of the bench. The vice was circular with two halves that met and overlapped in the middle. A long handle that was connected to the vice was pulled towards you. All that was needed was for the men to pick up two handfuls of sticks creating a bunch. You then chapped the bunch of sticks on the bench before placing them in the circular vice.

You then made sure your bunch was tight before you reached to the back of the vice and pulled forward the compression lever towards your body. The lever in turn crushed the sticks tightly. At the same time you reached out with your free hand and pulled a strand of string from an old mooring rope that had been cut to size so to encircle the bunches of sticks. Double knot the string and then release the long metal tension handle and there it was, a "Bunch of Glasgow Sticks". Tightly bound and every stick so evenly matched that a laser beam could not fault, my Da and his colleagues churned these out for a daily wage.

By the time you have read those few sentences my Da would have bunched and tied six to ten bunches of sticks, all perfect. The smell of the resin from cut logs and the different types of timbers will always stay with me. My Da, along with the working atmosphere, and his workmates who were making a fuss about me, saw me protesting to my Ma when she wanted to take me home (she had probably only been there to get my Da's wage). The camaraderie and the work ethic of these men who worked hard have had an effect on me to this day.

Their "patter" and laughter that filled the air from when I went in till I came out was tangible (even to a child) as it was good. Work satisfaction is an ethic I have always aimed for and have enjoyed most of my working life.

I remember when I was ten/eleven years old and we had moved from the Gorbals to Temple, my Da found this same type of work to help supplement his growing family. He was paid five shillings (25p) per gross which is 144 bunches of sticks, and he would do six gross per day for £1.50p. Even at my young age I was an expert at chopping sticks (even faster than my Da) and I would go into the wood yard (Wetherspoons) and cut him wood even when he was not there. I probably was the quickest at it, so I guess it was one apprenticeship I excelled at.

Self-pity

I have put these few paragraphs in due to the realisation that the children of today get thoughts and feelings of a changing world that none of the past generations have had to deal with.

Around eight years old I was in our home (grounded) and rummaging through the "scullery" (kitchen) drawers and shelves. Standing on our large kitchen table I then went through all the bric-a-brac that had been thrown up and on to the shelf that ran high around the kitchen walls. I came across a number of pills and the thought came to my mind about dying. I remember thinking about how to get back at the discipline I was now serving and decided to take the pills. This was my first serious encounter with self-pity, it was also the night where the Lord saw me through the physical turmoil that I brought on myself. It let me feel the love and concern my mum and dad had for me as I awoke in excruciating pain. I was in bed for twenty four hours and the doctor didn't know what the problem was.

Fortunately, I made a full recovery and never told anyone and thought nothing of it till my later years when I realised the power of "self-pity." Another realisation was the full force of love that came from my loving parents.

2

A New House

1954-1960

My Uncle Pat, who was the youngest child and only son, with five sisters on my mother's side, and my Da had been going on to me about the new house in Tambowie Street, Knightswood.

"It has got a bath" and "it is so far away, it will take ages to get there" were a couple of the comments I remember spoken by my two guardians as we boarded the number 2 bus heading to view our new proposed home.

To me as a child, it was the biggest adventure ever possible. There I was in between two men that I loved more than anything, and they were giving me all the attention, and time, to explain something exciting, even though I thought I was heading for a new planet rather than a new home.

It's only now that I can understand my Da and Uncle Pat's excitement, for we were heading for a two bedroom house with an inside toilet that would accommodate six of our family (my uncle Pat would become our first lodger).

We were moving out of a "single end" room and into a real home. As we climbed the stairs to the top deck of the number 2 bus I could hear my Uncle Pat say, "Go on John, I've got them here, let him try one!" "Pat, you will get me done in," came my father's response as he shook his head at his brother-in-law. "Okay, okay but just the once, and you better not let his Ma know," my Da continued.

I remember so clearly my Uncle Pat's laughter as he pulled out the *Woodbine* packet as soon as the conductor had taken our fare and returned to his station on the bottom deck. Apparently, as a child I had always walked about the house pretending to smoke anything that resembled a cigarette. Well, here was my big day. All I can remember, and remember well, was the laughter from my two protectors as they sat on the back seat of the bus behind me, watching as I puffed away until my heart was contented on my first *Woodbine* cigarette.

In today's climate both of them would be held in very low esteem and probably reported for child neglect, but to me it was a serious bonding that gave me a sense of closeness to a family who loved me.

I was assured (many years later by my dear late Uncle Pat who was one of the most caring men I knew) that I was none the worse for my experience and the cause for their laughter was that I did not cough once as they tried to remove the cigarette from my protesting small fingers. He also told me that I did not give up my "fag" without a fight. I was around four years old.

That was phase one of a trip I remember well as we got off the bus at Great Western Road to walk to Tambowie Street. It was a beautiful sunny day, not only the weather but also the expectation.

Skipping up that street while taking the hands of my Da and my Uncle Pat I was aware of how clean and bright the buildings looked and how each garden (yes, a garden) had a hedge or a fence.

At the top of the street was a high, red bricked wall that secured the privacy of the IOCO Ltd rubber works which manufactured products from electrical insulation to adhesive tape to varnishes.

This felt so good, and then it became even better when I realised that the three of us were going to sleep on the floor of our new house. My Ma and my two wee sisters would be arriving the following day.

So there I was in the middle of an amazing adventure, snuggled up on the wooden floor with blankets (made up like a bed), and in between the two men I knew would protect me if any impending danger dared to raise its head. What a day that had been; my first real cigarette, my first real home with a toilet, my first real sense of importance, and my first job as a security guard with my male relatives while we waited on the rest of our female family to arrive.

With starting a new school (St Ninian's) the following year and having the best play area in Glasgow meant that I was as happy and delighted with life as any child could be. On writing this book I have had a flood of memories from my primary school but one incident came to the fore.

It was raining and that meant we children had to play on the covered exterior wooden corridors. I can remember our group talking about foreign languages and being a show off I declared that I could speak in another tongue, which I did with no problem, except that I could not repeat the same words over again when asked to do so. What I can remember is feeling comfortable in the words I used. Now as a Christian I have been blessed with the gift of tongues. This is just a passing thought that I find interesting as an older man.

We had *Hunters* (a scrap metal iron works which we played in at night when it was closed) alongside *Robertson & Dunn* (timber mill) a canal, the bluebell woods, pitch and putt, hundreds of apple trees (these were not for public consumption but that did not deter us). The jewel in the crown was the five full sized football parks that were all on our doorstep.

Every place was an outlet to burn up excess energy along with an adventurous landscape that made Temple a great place to live. Added to this were the wonderful neighbours that any family would find easy to settle into.

Wake up call! Separation and hardship at Biggart's Residential Home

With having two young sisters, and there being just over three years between us, my Ma and Da where hard pressed in making ends meet.

We also had a new baby sister about to make her appearance into our family any week coming. So getting a chance to put us into a residential home was something our parents must have felt would have benefited us, as well as giving them a well-earned break.

I remember standing in Central Station, Glasgow, with a bunch of kids destined for the same residential home. Biggart's Residential Home (near Prestwick) was an establishment that had no real vocation towards children's welfare as we know it. Being such a young age (seven) I was always of the opinion that I must have been the problem due to the way I, and my sisters, were treated there. But recent revelation (with the aid of the internet) showed me that we were not alone in the treatment meted out to a lot of the children in this establishment.

On arrival at the home I was placed into a different wing from my sisters due to age and gender. After a week or so I asked if I could go and see them (just a walk along the corridor). I was kept waiting (I don't know if it was the same day or the next) before they took me to be with them for an hour. This was to be my only highlight in the time I was there.

Dinner time was a depressing time for me; creamed rice, semolina, tapioca or butter beans all meant force feeding, as I found out I could not eat any of this type of food without retching. A tablespoon of *Cod Liver Oil* and a red substance were given every morning too, which I managed to keep down. I tended to feel sick when these foods and oils were put before me so it became a ritual that when I refused to eat or was sick, it was just spooned back into my mouth by the two female supervisors in attendance. One would hold my arms behind me while the other held my head back with one hand as she force fed me through my clenched teeth with her other hand. This procedure was also used on one of my young sisters, so dinner time was an anxious time for both of us. To this day I still cannot eat any of these foods. It was a nightmare stay, not only being force fed but being kept from my two siblings.

I remember Christmas at the children's party, singing carols as we all sat on the floor. The party must have been in a local hall for I can remember we had to sing a song *(the words went something like…Here we are again at the Biggart's Home, happy as can be…)* on our way back in the bus provided. I remember every one of the staff were upbeat and seemed to want us to show our gratitude by being happy. We all wore paper hats and balloons were aplenty, but I was so unhappy (and felt that all the other kids were the same). It was like being force fed feelings, by saying, "You are going to enjoy yourself even though you are the unhappiest children in the world."

Even at this party I was still separated from my two wee sisters, who sat at the other side of the hall. My Ma came to see us just after that, and we put up such a protest (mostly crying, loudly) begging our Ma to take us home. We were distraught. I remember my Ma asking to speak to the matron who came into the visiting room. After my Ma informed the matron that she was taking the three of us home, there seemed to be a pregnant pause before the irate uniformed official informed my Ma (in front of us) that that was not happening.

Like a sergeant major she dictated the residential home's policy about resident children and informed my Ma that we would settle down and that it would be best for her to leave as soon as possible. We dreaded that she might be persuaded and obey this authoritarian matron. A cacophony of cries and wails hit my mother's ears as she interpreted our pleas, as "Ma, don't leave us, PLEASE."

"Oh is that right?" said my Ma quietly as she faced up to the official tyrant. "Well, I will show you what I can or cannot do matron," said my mum with words that lifted our hearts. "I will show you what is acceptable and not acceptable," my Ma continued. "Look at the state of my kids! Please get my children's clothes; I am taking them home with me right now!" For a few seconds I felt I was in a suspended animation vacuum as we waited on the matron's response. Now we all loved our Ma, but this one decision by a mother who stood up to a strict and cruel regime had sent her higher in our estimation than the stars. As far as we were concerned she was not only our parent she was also our hero.

My Ma had stood up to a matron, to a cruel regime and to the establishment just for us, wow, what a parent. Our train journey home was bliss and I remember even as a child thinking, "I can repay this by being good," aye right. On the way back to Glasgow we three kids stuck to our darling mother like limpets.

Although these residential schools were meant for good (and I have heard good reports of many of them too), it was probably the worst time I have ever spent in all my years of incarceration. It was the first time I had been forcibly separated from my two wee sisters even though they were both just at the other end of a corridor.

A religious experience

I think it is worth mentioning that my first serious desire (officially) to serve the Lord came when I was around eight years old. One of the altar boys at St Ninian's Chapel (the church I attended) was leaving the area so a vacancy must be up for grabs, or so I thought. I heard about this at school and was filled with a wonderful feeling of becoming a real servant of the Lord, by becoming an altar boy.

Not a word did I say to anyone as I ran home from school in record breaking time (well for me anyway). No one was at home and our key was always tied with a string behind the letter box. So as I ran into the house I was pulling off my school shirt, sort of rubbed my face without soap (well this was important) and was outside the house within five minutes of entering it. I did not care that the clean shirt I had put on was not ironed, nor did I give a hoot that my two knees were "manky" from being the goalkeeper at playtime in school.

I was so glad to see the chapel open as I hurried up the few steps towards the foyer.

"Right Patrick, what do you want in here at this time?" came the firm but gentle Irish accent from the strict priest, Father Murphy, who stood just inside the foyer at the church entrance.

"Ach Father Murphy," I said, allowing myself the feeling of relaxation (well we were going to be working together) as I stepped into the church to face him. "I heard that one of your altar boys was leaving the church and I was looking to see if I could get his job," I continued expectantly, believing I was the first applicant for the vacancy.

"Outside," he said, with no words but by indication of his head. So there I was, walking outside with the priest, totally secure that my first part of the interview had been a success, well I did not intend to seek a salary.

Father Murphy closed the large main church door behind us and said, "Stand here," pointing to the door that he had just closed. He slightly bent over, looked into my eyes, and said in a soft voice, "You will never serve Mass, you will never be an altar boy."

Now I know people will think that he was insensitive, to say the least, but I respected Father Murphy even though that may not have been reciprocated. Respected him so much that I believed him.

Not only did I respect him, but I revered him, and his strong Irish accent somehow reaffirmed to me that he was a godly man of the cloth – which he was. So there were two things to add to his quick decision on an eight-year-old boy's ambition, firstly, I was not crushed (but it did shape my spiritual outlook) and secondly, even though I was disappointed I put on a brave face and took it in my stride. Thankfully, as this had been a confidential interview, for nobody knew I was applying for the vacancy, nobody knew that I had had a knock back by way of a refusal.

Later on, after Father Murphy had predicted that I could only be one of the congregation, my young mind searched for some reason why I did not come up to God's standard and why I could not serve Him the way I saw others serve Him.

Oh, I loved God and I knew that I wanted to do something for Him, but how could I get round this setback, even at that tender age? Well, our church teachings came to my rescue as I thought up a spiritual deal concerning my salvation.

Purgatory

What a place. But it was a place I would aim for, for most of my life. I had been taught that souls that were not quite up to the spiritual mark would go to purgatory for a time before prayer got them released.

We on earth could pray for these souls and that would assist that release mechanism for them to go on and into heaven at a later time. I prayed, and in that prayer I decided that I would dedicate prayer and penance *"for the souls of the faithfully departed"* for the rest of my life. In turn, when I got to purgatory – that was now my main goal as I knew I was not going to get straight into heaven – I expected those same souls who had made it to heaven (and who I had prayed for) to pray for me, thus activating a release button for myself.

As an eight-year-old child I felt I had made not a bad compromise by giving up heaven for purgatory in the hope that with a bit of patience I, too, could reach my ultimate goal.

While I had not been able to swing the "altar boy job" I felt that this new purpose of prayer, and outlook, could put me in a place of still serving the Lord. It seemed like a good deal to me (I did another deal many years later just before I got saved, but we will come to that later), so I supposed that Father Murphy had been best intended but maybe he should have put it a tad gentler. I am sure if he was still with us today he would agree.

There is another point worth sharing regarding our church, it was a while later from being told that my altar boy application had been refused. I was supposed to go through Confirmation at St Ninian's, however, while getting ready for this event at home, I had fallen out with my Ma and refused to be confirmed, point blank.

My Ma was affronted, and dragged me up to the chapel, but I held my ground and refused to enter St Ninian's Church. So there I was, being confronted by Father Murphy and Father Mone and being asked why I did not want to be confirmed. Not only that, but I was standing at the same doorway where I had been refused the altar boy job.

By this time I was in too deep. How could I say that falling out with my Ma and being in a bad mood was the main and only reason I would not be confirmed? So I used all the wisdom I could muster; I kept quiet.

Many years later I was told by my Ma that the priests thought I had refused the sacrament of Confirmation because I had not been to confession (that would have made me ineligible for Confirmation) and apparently they thought I had done well to refuse the Confirmation Sacrament.

What I am about to write is what my mother told me about this incident…She said that Father Mone (who was later created Auxiliary Bishop of Glasgow by Pope John Paul II) said that this refusal by me had been spoken about in the Vatican. Calm down, calm down…apparently it was spoken about by Father Mone to other clergy when he was visiting the Vatican. My silence had paid dividends, much to my embarrassment as Father Mone was one of the gentle giants in the church.

I actually did in time become an altar boy, not only an altar boy but a "Head Altar Boy". Father Murphy did not know what he had missed. In St Joseph's and St Mary's approved schools I was head altar boy and could serve Mass in Latin which was used in those days.

In St Joseph's Approved School (Tranent, East Lothian) I would serve Mass seven days a week at 6am every morning (except Sundays which was at 10am). This was a school that had serious child abuse issues which would be brought to court many years later (by others boys).

I served Mass to at least one of those main abusers who attended these services daily. In St Mary's approved school (Bishopbriggs, Glasgow) I also served at the altar (Benediction and Mass once a week).

So just to put a cap on this and show you how our Lord works, I was finally confirmed by a man I served as an altar boy for at St Joseph's Approved School. He came once a month to serve Mass and his name was Archbishop Gray. He always took an interest in what I was doing and how my family were when he came to serve Mass.

One day, he asked if I had been confirmed and when I said no, he went out of his way and made arrangements for me to go to St Andrew's in Edinburgh where I was confirmed by this lovely Archbishop in a ceremony with only a few participants.

He saw the heart of a child and did something about it. Archbishop – later to become Cardinal – Gray made me feel special. (I was twelve-years-old at the time).

So one priest said I would never serve Mass and look what God did.

3

Glasgow Crime Wave

November 7, 1961

This date will always be etched in my mind for it started by me appearing at court in Glasgow. It was the day my childhood ended. Three of us (I was 11-years-old, my two pals were 10 and 13) stood accused of breaking into a wooden *Air Force Cadet* hut and making a mess.

The hut had been used for years by young boys from affluent districts of Glasgow, and even though the hut stood in our area, it was not for our group or class, not that that was an excuse for the vandalism we caused.

"You will be sent to St Joseph's Approved School for an indefinite period," were the words that rang out from the judge. Make no mistake about it, I knew that I deserved the sentence, and I also knew that I would not be shown any leniency by the court, but what on earth did "indefinite period" mean? This seemed to bother me more than where I was going to be sent to serve my time.

One of my pals, who was 13-years-old, came to St Joseph's with me while our other co-accused was sent to another establishment in Stirling.

They were heavy sentences for three kids, but we took it like men, much to our parent's grief, besides I had to put on a brave face because I had done time, for at 11-years-old I had form, petty yes, but form none-the-less.

My first venture into crime had been four/five years prior when our wee gang managed to wrench up the side of a wooden garage door and crawl through to the area that held the prize of a real ice cream van. To our dismay, no ice cream was kept in the van's fridge and the stock of sweets had been removed, but there were plenty of bottles of Irn Bru. They were the first fruits of my first misdemeanour.

We were never caught for this theft but time caught up with me when I confronted my Ma. Running along the railway track that backed on to the pilfered garage, I could not wait to give my mother the two bottles of Irn Bru that I had stolen (I think I had stashed the other three or four bottles in a safe place). Big mistake. No matter how much I tried to persuade my Ma that big boys had done it, and I had just picked up the bottles, she refused to accept them and to confirm this she gave me such a belt that I began to doubt that she could possibly be my mother.

One lesson I learned about this episode was not to tell my Ma anything regarding skulduggery. So from the great Irn Bru hoist to being sentenced to St Joseph's Approved School I had had three or four petty convictions (one was for playing football in the street, honest, my Da was fined £3). This was over a period of the four years.

During that time I received probation and was given two custodial sentences of 14 days detention (27th August 1959) and then 28 days detention (31st December 1959). The latter of those sentences was for breaking a deferred sentence.

Both sentences were carried out in Larchgrove Remand Home. You might be able to understand how by the time I was eleven I fully accepted the punishment of the courts, for I had not experienced leniency from judges or from the police, and I expected none.

Within that period I had run ins with the police, so leniency was a word not in my vocabulary regarding authority. I was obviously a wee "skunner" to the authorities.

My first visit to Larchgrove Remand Home

My first run in with the police face to face had a profound effect on my attitude to authority, not just physically but mentally too.

At the time it was just one of those things that happen (probably just a misdemeanour that could have been sorted by reporting me to my parents), but on reflection it gives me the insight to see the starting point of my dislike and rebellion to authority and the police in particular. It also helps me to understand where the dislike started and where I went right off the track.

Now Larchgrove Remand Home was a new establishment opened in 1957 for juvenile offenders. My first visit to this establishment saw me sitting in the back of a police car beside a large policeman and listening to the two officers in the front seat.

"What time is it?" asked one of the officers. "Oh, we have an hour to go," replied his colleague who was driving.

"So what do you think? Do we take him to his home or drop him off at the Remand Home?" inquired the first officer in a manner that I thought was just to scare me.

But he was serious, my future attitude to authority hung in the balance as I awaited the outcome of the conversation that was taking place.

The officer sitting beside me then joined in when he said matter of factly, "Let's take him to Larchgrove, I have not been in there and it will be good to have a look around this new place."

I can't remember what crime I had committed to deserve such attention or what made the officers take me to a unit at the other side of the city when it was obvious that they had the option of taking me home. Anyway, there I was, eight years old and just making the deadline to be booked into the Remand Home as the boys had been showered and put to bed.

My guards were shown around the new building as I was booked in and then showered alone. With damp hair, new clean pyjamas, towel, Gibb's toothpaste and a toothbrush I was led down the dark corridor that was dimly lit by a red light. At the end of the corridor, which housed the dormitories, I was led into one of the dormitories that held six/eight boys. This room too had a red light that gave an eerie sense of heaviness. All the boys in the room seemed to be sleeping so I had no one to answer any of my inquiries or comfort my worries.

I could only think about my Ma as I lay on the starched sheets of the single metal framed bed. What would she say? What would she think? Did she know where I was? What were my three wee sisters thinking and would they be missing me? Would I ever get out? It was the first time I had been away from my loving parents and sisters.

I felt so alone and so vulnerable but I couldn't shed any tears from my moist eyes because the thought of anyone knowing that I was crying would have been too much to bear. I think this is where I learned to cry inwardly.

My nightmare had only begun as I awoke (a couple of hours later) to find that I had wet the bed. I could not even remember going to sleep but there I was with damp sheets and pyjamas.

"Oh no," was my first thought, "how do I get out of this?" The embarrassment far outweighed any loneliness, rejection or self-pity, this was a crisis and that crisis came under the Glasgow banner of "Ridicule" or in short "A Riddy".

"Thank God it is still dark and everyone is still asleep," was my first thought and the only consolation at the disaster that had struck me. I knew there would not be enough time to get the bed dry with body heat alone. Who on earth could have thought that wetting the bed would be an antidote for homesickness, rejection and despair?

Well, all thoughts of my incarceration predicament left me as I scanned the dormitory for a hot radiator that would come to my assistance. There were no radiators to be seen in the dull glow of the red light, and then I noticed that on one of the walls (without beds and just above the floor), two four inch heating pipes ran the full length of the room.

What a result, quickly and quietly I pulled off my sheet and wrapped it around the hot pipe knowing it would not take long to remove the dampness.

So there I was, having come through one of the most traumatic and emotional experiences (all my own doing) in my young life feeling relieved as my sheet and pyjamas were on their way to being fully restored back to their arid state.

"Are you ok?" came a whisper from the corner of the room. "Oh no," was all I could think – I thought I had got away with it as I saw a boy about my age coming towards me.

"Sheets wet?" he asked without any sarcasm. "I have used the pipes too," he said sympathetically as he came and sat beside me on the hot pipe.

I don't know what we spoke about in the childish whispers but that child and a wet bed got me through my first night of imprisonment in a place that would become known for its child abuse.

Even now, I am aware that in such trivial events as these may seem, our Lord has a word that says *"I will never leave you or forsake you."*

That wee boy who sat beside me was an angel that saw me through my first night of separation from my family, and it took a wet bed to do it. Not only an angel but quite a good lawyer, too, as he explained what the court procedure would be for me. How neat.

Who knows what would have happened had those three officers taken me home? What I do know is that the work I am doing now, is in part, because of that decision. It started my apprenticeship that no school or university can teach, and I thank our Lord for the path that I have taken, for it was a path leading me straight to Him. It's a path where I can understand what being locked up means, and it is also a revelation of those I hurt, victims and family.

4

St Joseph's and 'The Brothers'

St Joseph's Approved School, Tranent, East Lothian
Date of sentence: November 7, 1961
Sentence: Indefinite period
Released: May 15, 1963 (St de La Salle day)

There are many things in life we are not proud of, and on occasion some things that we arc embarrassed about and I am no different from the next man, but I would like to take a bit of time on this part of the story.

St Joseph's Approved School was a nightmare for the boys in the institution that was run by "Brothers" of the religious order of St de La Salle. There were six of these men (Brothers Peter, Aloysius, Patrick, Bernard, Lawrence and Sebastian), they also had several staff members (civilian) in support.

On admission I was the youngest boy in the school that held 80 residents whose ages ranged from thirteen to sixteen. I should have gone to St Ninian's in Stirling but because of a shortage of placements for my age I was sent to St Joseph's in Tranent instead.

Myself and one of my co-accused were driven to East Lothian by my probation officer, Mr Irvine, (oh yes, I forgot to mention that I was already on probation).

Mr Irvine was a gentleman who took his job seriously and with compassion. He had a heart for those under his charge. He was from Aberdeen and many years later, in 1967, he would secure a two week trial trip at sea for me with the *Woods Deep See Fishing Trawler Company* as a deckhand.

So the drive to our destination was pleasant and relaxed. Mr Irvine handed us over to the headmaster, Brother Peter, before he was taken into the office for tea and biscuits

The building itself was intimidating and when we were left alone with the headmaster it was obvious that he was the boss and he let us know as his voice changed when out of the presence of Mr Irvine

A book could be written on this subject alone so I will just allow you to see what the children of this home were put through by a cruel regime.

After getting settled in to the home I had a deep experience that I thought I would not be able to bear. I would like to share with you this feeling of sickness that made me cry out to the Lord. It was a silent cry and it was done in a bed in a dormitory that held just over twenty boys.

My bed was beside a large window and it was very late into the night that had a full moon. I remember the prayer so well and it was the high point of grieving as if I had lost my family forever. Although I had only just arrived at St Joseph's, I was a boy who had previous convictions, and someone with "previous" should be used to being "put away."

Silent tears were only a reflection of the deep pain that crippled my stomach. I made not a sound (nor could I, at the expense of being found out by my peers) as I held the corner of my pillow tight to my mouth.

"Lord," I prayed as exhaustion pressed in on me, "let time pass," was my cry and my prayer. They were my last words as I allowed my eyes to close and cut out the light from the bright moon. I fell into a deep sleep, but when I awoke the same feeling of despair, although subsided slightly, was still there.

I could not eat at breakfast and I reported to the matron to tell her I was not well. She immediately moved me into the small two bed sick bay for a day or two and she informed me that I was suffering from "Home Sickness."

I had never heard of this before but the prognosis sounded right. I don't know if it was a physical ailment or not but I do know that my child like spirit was crushed at being separated from my family.

I felt totally alone, even among 80 boys, and I experienced deep concern and trauma. (The only thing to have matched this was the birth of my son Barclay, but we will come to that later).

Having said all this and the state I was in I believe the Lord heard my prayer and granted me sleep that night at the point where I thought my heart would stop. He would not allow me to be broken.

Not being able to share with anyone about my "childish behaviour" I went into this sentence with all these feelings well and truly buried and not for public scrutiny from my inmates. Only One person could release me from this, but that again is for later.

At the hands of the 'Brothers'

Brother Patrick always seemed angry, and going into the dining room while he was on duty was a dangerous hazard if you erred in the slightest. When entering the dining room there had to be silence. Once everyone was seated, all 80 boys, four to a table, and grace was said, the member of staff clapped their hands which started a loud roar of conversation and the sound of cutlery on plates.

Once the meal was finished, a clap of the hands reactivated the silent mode. At this point we had to sit back and fold our arms as we waited for all 20 tables to be cleared by a couple of staff, but usually by the boys, and that could last up to fifteen minutes.

Brother Patrick would hover in and out of the tables looking for someone to break the silent curfew. With his arms folded and his hands hidden inside his black cassock sleeves we all knew that he had an offensive weapon hidden up his wide sleeve, usually a heavy, boned handled butter knife. He would hold the blade in his hand and use the boned handle, with force, on the head of anyone who dared to be a curfew breaker by a laugh or a sound.

It may sound strange but it was funny to us kids (as long as it was not us being the subject of attack). The danger from a Brother Patrick attack would be when he was at the back of you. We sat four to a table and when the dear brother was walking behind you, you grimaced as you awaited a blow to connect with your head.

If you were to be reprimanded by a bone handle, that was acceptable, but the fright of the sudden attack made boys shout out all sorts of phrases, like, "Oh Mammy, Daddy". But once he passed you could breathe easy.

It then became the turn of the boys facing you, for when he walked behind those boys you could see all the different kinds of grimacing and fear on your fellow inmates faces. That was funny. This was dangerous because, even though it was funny, sometimes extremely funny, you dare not make a sound or Brother Patrick would do a second circuit and he missed few who broke the house rule of silence.

On occasion, blood did flow.

Brother Patrick was a strict man who thought nothing of using his knuckles on the heads of us kids for all sorts of things, maybe deserved, but the punishment always seemed harsh.

Then we had Brother Bernard and Brother Lawrence, who I felt cared about us but both had tempers that could flare up in an instant. In fairness to these men they had a band of boys who could be unruly to say the least, but violent chastisement was used by Brother Bernard.

Brothers Bernard and Lawrence taught in their classrooms and Bernard had a passion for bagpipes. He took bagpipe and drum classes and had outside volunteers who were excellent pipers and drummers to come and help teach. I joined his class and even managed to learn a few tunes on the old blow bag, much to my delight.

St Joseph's had a pipe band and they carried out gigs for different events. I was taken along to a few of them dressed in our full band uniform, kilts and all.

Because I was a learner I was allowed to keep the drones operating but the reed was taken out of the chanter and the chanter blocked by a slate nail, I was twelve at the time. By doing this I was allowed to participate silently with the band at outside gigs, (I think Brother Patrick would have appreciated the bagpipes being silent). It was a great thrill to be part of the band and I am grateful to Brother Bernard for that.

On reflection I not only learned about bagpipe music I was also introduced to playing cricket, which I still enjoy watching.

In the three workshop Annexes we had a tailors, a woodworkers and metal craft. I was allowed to use all the tools and machinery in each department, even at my young age.

One of the highlights for me was when I was given permission to make a pair of long corduroy trousers (school code was short trousers). It took me a while but by the time I was finished I had mastered the sewing machine, thanks to the patience of old Mr Rooney. This would stand me in good stead as I used this sewing skill during most of all of my future incarcerations. So even at my young age I was the only boy wearing long trousers in St Joseph's.

One of the serious enjoyments I had was the school's four grass football parks where the goals had nets – indulgence indeed.

There was a good young man on the staff, not much more than 19, whom we all liked, his name was Brother Sebastian. He wore *Brylcreem* hair gel and pointed shoes with side laces under his cassock. He always had a laugh and a joke for the boys, no matter how young or old. The whole school was upset when we learned he had suddenly left without saying goodbye. Apparently he had left at night when we all had been put to bed, so the rumour went.

There was another male teacher who came to work with us, and our class were merciless with this man. I used to feel sorry for him. He had a good leather briefcase on his first day in class and someone saw that it was his daughter Sally who had put her name inside the flap. That was his nickname for the rest of the time he was there, Sally. I was always pleased to see that he laughed it off.

I had a bullying problem from the time I entered the school. An older lad, Colin (14), never took to me and I paid for it. Never giving into him I would always fight back.

On one occasion he came up to me from behind and kicked me on the thigh with his hob nailed boot. The pain was so excruciating as I collapsed onto the playground yard. I could not stop the fall as a tsunami of self-pity and anger engulfed me. As I lay there helpless with tears of rage in my eyes my thoughts somehow turned towards my parents and family, whom I missed so much. This made me angrier, so much so that I rose and hobbled after my antagonist, only to hear him laughing as I attempted to retaliate.

We had a number of run ins but each time I would never back down, in fact I was getting closer to overcoming him. On our last confrontation in a classroom, (I was a big 13 now), Colin decided to back down when I once again faced him up. Without a blow I knew that I had won our long acrimonious confrontations. It was a relief rather than a victory. I was just glad it was over.

Over the many years of incarceration I used to look out for Colin, but our paths never crossed again.

I think it worthy of note to write about one other experience I had. Every year the school went to Forfar to pick berries. We were housed in wooden army type huts, Brother Peter's caravan was just outside the hut we slept in.

One sunny afternoon (we had to take a nap after lunch) I was fooling around outside with a wee pal when Brother Peter came rushing out of his caravan with his house coat on and his wispy hair ruffled.

He let out a roar, "Clark, in here, now!"

I was struck silent and rooted to the ground as my guardian reached for me and dragged me up and into his caravan. His face was scarlet as he raged about the noise I had been making outside his abode. He then grabbed his belt with his free hand as he continued to rag doll me with his other.

The inside of the caravan seemed cluttered as he took a couple of swipes at me with a belt that was an offensive weapon. Then just as quickly as I had been taken in, I was miraculously pushed out of the caravan and released.

This should have been a great victory for me as a twelve-year-old, but instead of being humble and grateful to have escaped the clutches of an angry man, I made a silly comment to my wee pal who seemed not to have moved from the spot since I had been kidnapped by the middle aged cleric. The bravado words of "nae problem" were not even out of my mouth when I was once again dragged into the lion's den (camouflaged as a caravan) by Brother Peter who had not even locked his door before I voiced my verbal kamikaze statement.

As I was being belted the second time (not as badly as expected, due to the confined lack of space) I happened to look into the corner of the caravan where the bed was – the blankets were in disarray, but I noticed movement just before one of my fellow inmates (about the same age as me) popped his head and bare shoulders from under the covers, it was evident he was naked.

I had disturbed our headmaster in his intimacy with one of the schools boys. On reflection I think this young boy might have saved me from more serious punishment had he kept out of the way. I don't know if the belting was sore, as the fear of Brother Peter exceeded anything a leather strap could inflict on me. The bruised welts left evidence of what Brother Peter had done to me. I had seen that same strap belt on one of our senior boys who had absconded and was always ready to stand up to the staff.

Big Chesney – our hero

He was our hero. Big Chesney was called up in front of us (at night assembly) and we were told by Brother Peter that Chesney was going to get six of the best from this same black leather strap that I had had the encounter with.

A pair of silk tartan shorts were handed to him (as was every time corporal punishment was inflicted, except at my time in the caravan), which he was ordered to put on (this was compulsory for punishment).

He was then taken into our large shower room adjacent to the recreation room. The acoustics in this room would do as an echo chamber for the headmaster to show us inmates how misbehaviour was treated as he would attempt to break our friend and hero.

The shower door was left open for full effect (where I stood in my line up I could also see into the shower room) as the first whack from the leather strap met the backside of big Ches. To a boy we prayed, "Don't cry big man, don't cry, and don't give in."

No sooner had the acoustic explosion of leather on flesh echoed around the shower room when the elongated cry from Ches penetrated into our souls. The sound of his pain was not one of fear but of defiance and anger.

"Aaaggghhh!" he had screamed louder and longer than he had to, as he held his backside while running forward for a few steps.

I could see Brother Peter's face grow red as our big hero turned and defiantly stepped back to face his assailant. Slowly he turned his back to the headmaster and bent over to receive more pain from a guardian who was not able to show compassion.

"Thwack!" came the punishing sound that we felt would break us all, but once again big Ches went through the same routine.

"He is not going to make it," we thought. He must break at the power being unleashed on him. We knew what was happening, our friend was going to break down and cry and ask for mercy, that was the purpose of this public flogging. It was also to show us that Brother Peter was in control.

Six of the best big Chesney got and six of the best big Chesney took, and to our delight he never shed a tear. Our headmaster was furious as he shouted to his staff to get us all to our dormitories.

A couple of days later our hero spent a lot of time in the toilets at break times. This ensured that every one of us was able to see the best that Brother Peter could give out as punishment. But it was still not enough to break the defiance of a young lad we were all proud of.

I can honestly say that when it was our turn to have a look at his welts of punishment, we thought big Chesney had a pair of old, dirty, dark, tartan shorts on. Outside of a Picasso, I had never seen such colours that came from bruising.

My own bruisings paled into insignificance to the kaleidoscope of colours that big Ches wore on his legs and backside.

So our hero now had the marks, welts and colours of a patriot, and even better, he didn't succumb to the intended breakdown that was planned for him.

Release day

On the morning of May 15, 1963, there was expectancy in the school. It was St de La Salle's holiday. On this holy day we got to play cricket, football and other such games. The food always went up a notch and the atmosphere was pleasant as was any "holiday of obligation."

That morning in the play yard I walked past Brother Peter, who seemed to be in his usual serene mood, when I heard him say, "How long have you been here, Clark?"

I looked up at him and said without hesitation, "Eighteen months, Brother." All I remember was him saying, "You are getting out today," as he walked past me.

Oh, I so wanted that to be true, but I could not allow myself to believe it as I nervously laughed. I really did not know if I had heard what he had said. I was in an unbelieving daze. Surely he would not be kidding me on?

Well if he wasn't, what do I do now? It was a couple of hours to lunch and it was a long time in passing.

After lunch I was called aside and told to go upstairs with one of the staff. Another couple of boys were being released along with me; even after I was dressed in my new suit and shoes I still did not believe it. I had not seen anyone released like this.

"It's just a joke," I kept telling myself. "Don't listen to what's been said," I kept repeating silently.

But it was not a joke, I was being released with brand new clothes and I was going home to my family, who were not aware of my release.

So when I walked up Tambowie Street late that afternoon with £1 17s 6d (£1.75p) in my pocket from the savings I had earned picking berries in the Forfar camp, l was a thirteen-year-old man.

It had only been nine short years prior to this that I had skipped up the same street holding my Da and Uncle Pat's hands, secure and full of expectation for the future.

Now here I was, immaculately dressed in my Italian suit with money in my pocket that I wanted to give to my Ma (I felt as if I was a provider).

My time was done, I was street wise and I could stand on my own two feet. But in my short journey to manhood there had been no direction for the path I was now on, no comforter to counsel or instructions to follow – only harsh words, bullying, confrontation, punishments and heartache of being away from a family that I cherished.

Dirty books and dirty talk were all part of growing up – I had witnessed violence and sex abuse. But that was okay, I knew how to deal with anything that would crop up. Or so I thought, for by this time I must have been a heartache to both my parents although they never once abandoned me. Little did I know that I would be in and out of institutions for the next twelve years.

That special freedom feeling

Believe me, one of the wonders of being incarcerated, from a nine-year-old kid to a 32-year-old man, is the day you walk away from imprisonment. From custody to freedom, the feeling is never surpassed. The birth of my children are on another plateau, of course, but the elation of freedom is fully experienced no matter what your age.

It is a special feeling that can only be described by those who have been released from a prison cell or incarceration. I was to go on and have many more of these "released experiences" from establishments and never once did I intend to, or want to go back.

Of course, these feelings are physical/emotional and they in turn never stay strong for once the honeymoon period, usually a couple of days to a couple of weeks, is over then everything goes back to the way it was.

This feeling never reaches the heights of revelation from the Lord Jesus Christ at the point where we are loosed from the bondage of sin. Sin sounds awfully religious, but it just meant my condemnation was finally removed from my conscience.

This is "true release" that lasts a lifetime and beyond, but we will come to that later on in the book. John 8:36 says *"So if the Son sets you free, you will be absolutely free."*

The man I became at thirteen was put in his place when our wee gang decided to let the Police know that they were not liked in our area. So rather than drop them a note we decided to use paint, mostly gloss, as we felt it would have a better effect on our local constabulary (by this time I was a vandal doing graffiti, disguised as protest).

Well, needless to say that I was arrested and taken into the Police Office where I told the arresting officer that my name was Donald Duck. I then refused to give my name, saying, "I can't remember."

Managing to keep this up for about three or four minutes I was advised to give my proper name when the large desk sergeant informed me that he had a deft interrogation method. Unrepentant, he took me into the police muster room and, with one kick, he gave me an aerodynamic flight that was made possible by a very large boot. As that propelled voyage came to an end he followed it up with a slap to the back of my head that sounded like an explosion.

I did not know what to hold first, my backside or the throbbing at the base of my skull. It's amazing what can restore your memory. No amnesia for this boy as I gave my name, rank and serial number. To my shame I went and complained to the authorities about my treatment but the case was found not guilty and that was okay with me, I wasn't even fourteen.

Before 1964 I was in trouble again. By the time my case reached court it was 1965 by which time I had spent a short period in a normal school, St Thomas Aquinas, even if it was for only a short period.

This time it was St Mary's Approved School in Glasgow that had been given the task of keeping me in order.

April 1964 to May 1965

I had been charged under *The Powers Act – The Prevention of Crime Act 1953 Section 1(1),* which sounds like espionage but no such adventure took place on the night of my arrest.

My wee pal and I decided to go to Stoats Dairies for jobs as milk delivery boys. Now Stoats Dairies paid two guineas (£2.10p) per week whereas Sloan's Dairies only paid £1 17s (£1.75p) a no brainer.

Sloan's Dairy were just around the corner from my house, but here was the bigger factor to take into account than wages – Stoats Dairies had horse drawn milk carts.

As I had worked in both establishments before I knew how good it was to go into the stables of Stoat's Dairies early in the morning (2.30 am) and see the horses being prepared for their day's work. Anyway, on the way to our intended destination to see about employment, we met two police officers.

They found that we had a torch in our possession but seemed to believe our genuine reason for being out and that we were going to Stoat's Dairies. Unknown to us however, they followed our journey. At this point I need to put up my hands, even though at the time I denied it to the two officers, we were flashing our torch into the rear windows of shops as we walked.

So although our sole intention was wholesome in seeking work, the temptation to see if anything could be gained on the way to that work would have been a bonus.

We did not touch or damage anything, just had a look as we passed by, but the *Powers Act* said that being out too late at night and acting suspiciously was enough.

Guilty as charged. Thirteen months in St Mary's Approved School.

I was now used to being away from my family, so this time there was no hassle in the approved school, although I did have one serious fight that was not reported but the outcome gave me relative peace for the rest of my sentence.

One thing I did dislike, like most folk (and it's the same today) and that is bullies. St Mary's for me was okay with plenty of football and the job satisfaction I got from the work I was allocated to.

I worked in the maintenance department doing all sorts of jobs from painting and decorating to plumbing and glazing. We even emptied the school's bins, it was a good number and I was allowed one day home leave every Sunday. With four weeks to go before I was released I was allowed to find an outside job.

I managed to secure employment with Johnston's Bakery, in Partick. This was heavy work and even though I was a strong young man, carrying one hundredweight sacks of flour up to the first floor from a delivery truck was just a bit too much, even for me.

I was still only fifteen and I was going back to the school each night exhausted even though the flour delivery was only once per week. So I made a decision that would sort out this problem. I decided to put my notice in at the bakery on the same day I was to leave St Mary's. It so happened that this was a Saturday morning (half day) as I finished my final shift and then returned back to St Mary's, only because the headmaster insisted I should go to work that final morning. He instructed me to then return to the home, pick up my saved wages, belongings and signing out forms.

What a hassle, but I was in control. I duly finished my shift, got my final wage packet and said cheerio to the bakers and staff for the last time.

History has a way of repeating itself, and not letting myself down, I messed up by opening my mouth and taking my foot out, again.

Back at the school I already had everything packed and as I was leaving the headmaster's office after signing the release papers, he asked if I was working on the Monday. I don't know if he knew that I had left the bakery for good that very same afternoon or not. But I could not lie to him and told him I had chucked it in that very day. He was not a happy bunny. It was like getting pulled back into the caravan in St Joseph's after being released, but without any physical violence this time.

So up the stairs I went, back to the same dormitory and bed I had left ten minutes before. My new instructions were fair and lenient as I was ordered to get another job on Monday morning or I was staying put in St Mary's indefinitely – I knew what indefinite meant by then. I think the headmaster tended to lean towards my side, although he did not say, regarding the heavy labour I was employed to do at the bakery.

I managed to get a job the following Monday at five shillings (25p) less. It was a small engineering works called JJ Neil's and was just a stone's throw from my home. It was a small storage factory which stocked parts for old Stoker Boilers.

While working in JJ Neil's I was with wee "Hocky" who was one of my pals. It was when gangs were all the go in Glasgow and we, like everyone else, wanted to start our own gang.

As youngsters we called ourselves the Tambowie Rebels but decided to go national and take in the population from the whole of Temple, one of the smallest districts in Glasgow.

I do need to say that the pals I had, and still have from Temple, were and are of the best quality. Good friends, loyal, and at the time, game for anything, in other words, we were just daft.

We decided to call our gang the "Scurvy." Now I don't think the name would get any nominations or awards for content but we liked it. An older generation before us had used the name "Scurvy" in Bar-L – Glasgow's Barlinnie Prison. We had known these men and we looked up to them. It was they who had influenced us to build our foundation on quicksand.

A dark night

It was one of those nights when we had made our way back to Tambowie Street from a gallivant up at the canal.

There were about six of us swaggering along with a couple of slug guns in our possession. Alas we had fired all our pellets to no avail, as we attempted to rid the planet of myxomatosis, so the slug guns were useless, besides it was dark by the time we reached our destination at the close mouth in Tambowie Street. It seemed a bit strange to us that night for the area was very quiet which was unusual for Tambowie Street. We had noticed a couple of men walking past separately with heads down, and in different directions.

A week prior to this our local shop had been burgled and a very large amount of cigarettes had been stolen.

I reached the close front and was standing talking to an older pal (Jack A) as our four other mates were making their own way towards us in twos. I heard a whistle blow and saw one of my pals in the distance running toward me as the other three disappeared over hedges and down the street.

"Polis" (police) was the cry that always made us stampede, even if we had done nothing wrong. Having a slug gun tucked in my trouser belt, then stampede, in my opinion would be a necessity.

The word "Polis" reminds me of when the wildebeest sees the lion and the herd run with all their might even before they turn their heads to see where they are going. So to us Scurvy boys the word "Polis" just meant "scatter!"

As I ran through the close I realised that my pal, Bosco, who had been the farthest away, had almost reached us, so I held back and let Jack A run past me into the darkness of the back court. Just as I put my head out of the close Bosco was about to run past me. "In here Bosco!" I shouted, as he swerved towards me, almost taking the sharp detour on his elbows. At the same time I turned and ran, with Bosco now close at my back.

Jumping down the backcourt steps in one bound saw me onto the rear backcourt pathway. We were just heading for the metal railings that fenced off each backcourt and clothes line drying area when I heard a skirmish and muffling sound to the side of us.

As I turned I could just make out, with the lights from living rooms on the tenement shining down, two male figures wrestling. Jack A had been captured by an unknown assailant when I had let him run past me to go back and see if Bosco was okay.

An older man was behind Jack A and had an arm lock around his throat as muffled noises escaped as he fought for breath.

"Let him go ya bam," was all I could think of as I walked closer to the fracas and an assailant who was obviously from another gang. Then, remembering I had my slug gun in my trouser belt, I pulled it out and pointed it at my pal's captor.

"Let him go," I repeated.

"Now son, don't be daft," came the reply from a man I had never seen or known, he was certainly not a neighbour from our area nor a rival gang leader.

"I am a police officer, so don't do anything stupid," he said as he struggled to keep his hold on Jack A. My first thought was that my slug gun (which could not penetrate cardboard, and didn't have any slugs) had no chance of getting Jack A free. I also knew that I was in deep trouble if this was the Polis and not a run of the mill assailant.

I got my opportunity to escape when I heard reinforcements rushing into the close we had just exited. With Bosco at my side we glanced at one another and ran in tandem towards the metal railing without saying a word.

We both vaulted this hurdle on one hand but as Bosco was always faster than me, he was three strides in front before he was flipped up into the air. It was like slow motion, one second he was running full pelt, the next he stopped in a horizontal position five feet from the ground (time stopped as he seemed to hang there for a split second) before thumping down onto the grass.

I helped him to his feet as he coughed and spluttered while holding his throat. "I never saw the rope," he rasped.

He had just run into a taut clothes line without any clothes to warn a casual jogger. It had stopped Bosco quicker in his tracks than any Polis could have.

Remembering that night and the seriousness of my actions, the disappointment of not being able to help Jack A, and wanting to laugh my head off at Bosco's misadventure on the trapeze was strange as I didn't know what the outcome would be.

I was never identified in this escapade and my pal Jack A never gave my name, so all I can think is that the plain clothed officer did not see my empty slug gun and even if he did he could not identify me.

A few of my friends were arrested that night and charged with a Breach of the Peace.

The biggest revelation of this act is that if that had happened in today's climate I probably would have been dealt with very differently, the Police quick response team would have made sure of that. So even in my stupidity I was protected.

From there on in I had a number of sentences; from Borstal right through Young Offenders and main stream prison (untried and convicted).

5

Wake Up Call! Borstal and Beyond

Incarcerated Again

Borstal training saw me serving thirteen months, at 16-years-old, for carrying an offensive weapon. That's what I got for helping to start up a gang, and deservedly so.

The strange thing about this was that Polmont Borstal in Falkirk was full at the time, so I was sent to Barlinnie's C Hall's untried building (Top Flat) instead of Borstal.

C Hall was a building that housed untried adult prisoners (over 21 years of age) who were locked up for 23 hours a day. The top flat of C Hall had been commandeered by the authorities and set aside, so that they could accommodate the overflow of Borstal boys (approximately 60 lads).

So once again I found myself one of the younger boys in a place of incarceration. I remember that sunny Friday night so well, it was a wakeup call to being seriously locked up.

After being in the main reception area for hours (in the dog box), where I had been showered and clothed with a clean mole skin uniform and ill-fitting prison shoes, I was then given sheets, blankets, towel and toiletries before I was marched through to the main prison and into C Hall.

On entering C Hall and looking up, I could see the glass roof high above me. There were three levels above ground (2nd, 3rd and 4th flats), with each level having a four foot passageway that ran the full length and breadth of C hall.

On each floor there was a central galley (about 10 feet wide) and stairway that was connected to each of the respective passages. These were the landings where two prisoner officers per landing ran their floor levels and security in conjunction with the desk at the C Hall entrance (where I now stood).

Standing at C Hall's reception desk for a while, trying to look as calm as I could in the middle of hustle and bustle as prisoners slopped out before being locked up for the night, I was finally told by the Principle Officer (PO) to make my way upstairs to the top flat.

With my bed sheets and pyjamas still held in my outstretched arms, I heard the order from the PO behind me, "One for the top," and before I had taken three steps I heard the echoing response "Right, sir," from somewhere high above me and deep in the hall.

It was all a bit surreal walking up the wooden stairway in silence, as prisoners were now all locked up. The fourth flat prison officer showed me to my accommodation in silence. It was cell number 4/43, which was just next to the slop out/ toilets and the central galley.

Without any comment or instruction he opened the cell door, stood to the side while still holding his key in the lock, he motioned for me to enter. I had no sooner entered the cell than the door was slammed and locked shut behind me.

I must have stood for a few seconds taking in what would be home for my foreseeable future.

I then sort of leaned backwards and rested against the steel door that had just been unceremoniously slammed shut at my back.

"Aye right," I thought as my mind raced back to the night I was in the police car waiting to see if I was going to Larchgrove Remand Home or not.

The cell itself was freshly painted in yellow but the newly painted "fumes" did not stand a chance with the rancid ammonia smell that impregnated the air, it was sickening. The shimmering aroma was coming from a fur lined "chanty pot" that sat in the corner like a metal plague.

It seemed to be lined with a green algae and it was an object that you would not want to use, even from a distance.

Looking up at the window that faced me it was recessed in the cell wall and was high enough to almost touch the ceiling but not low enough to see through.

This window was supposed to keep the rain and wind out and it failed on several points; each point being a broken or missing piece of glass in the old Victorian metal frame. Each of these panes were four inches square and the ones that were damaged or missing were stuffed with newspaper or cloth.

The metal bunk beds had two horse hair mattresses that were rolled up to the end of each bed. Both bunk beds supported the flimsy mattresses with thin strips of metal that were criss-crossed in an uneven pattern so as not to leave too big a gap at any one point. Some of the metal straps were tied with string which made up for the shortfall of the ones that were missing.

A wooden board that was hinged at the base was attached to the opposite wall from the beds. This was for any extra prisoners when accommodation got tight. To cap it off, the floor was made of stone and it reminded me of a pavement.

"Surely I'm not going to be left here?" my mind said, almost out loud.

I heard numbers being called from each landing as prison officers gave their prisoner number totals to the main desk on the ground floor. This was followed by footsteps running downstairs – then…silence.

I finally put my sheets and toiletries on the lower metal bed strips and went back to the door. Somebody is going to come soon and say to me, "Haha – only kidding," I thought. But they didn't, this was no mistake.

I learned something that night to my cost. I was so thirsty and there was a bell on my cell wall, so I pressed the bell and waited and waited. About an hour later while I was sitting on the bed frame (still unmade) the spy hole on the door flicked up.

"What do you want?" came the harsh words from a bodiless eye? Thinking he was there to serve and knowing he would understand that I had been put in the wrong place I said in my most humble voice, "I am thirsty."

The words were no sooner out of my mouth than I was told that the only time I pressed a cell bell was when I was dead. I was also informed to make sure I was dead, because if I was not dead I soon would be if he had to come in.

Lesson one; don't disturb prison officers on night shift, let dehydration take its course.

It's strange how the human body and mind buckles down to adversity, even at a young age. I read some books and I even made a paper football from old newspapers tied up with mailbag strings. I learned how to perfect "keepy up" in my cell, much to the annoyance of the older untried prisoners on the landing below me.

I was also taught how to sew eight stitches to the inch while making and repairing Royal Mail bags, a trade that would surely not catch on, nor ever become popular on the outside world.

Polmont

My three months, probably nearer to ten weeks, in Bar-L went by before I was moved on to Polmont Borstal, near Falkirk. I remember my first night in Polmont (another lovely evening) and being locked up in a clean and tidy cell room that had a wooden door.

I picked up the bible provided to each cell and I earnestly tried to read it, but no matter how I tried I could not concentrate or take any of the words in. I don't know if it was the wording (it was a King James translation) or not, all I knew was that no words were penetrating my mind.

I can honestly say that the timing for me to be "saved" was not in borstal for my Lord had an apprenticeship for me to fulfil. He had *"plans to prosper me and not to harm me, plans to give me hope and a future,"* Jeremiah 29:11. But borstal was not the place it would happen.

I also had a wee run in with a few of the borstal lads that were members of another gang. They knew my cousin, who was incarcerated in another hall of the borstal, and they let me know that they were out to get me because they saw him as their enemy.

It just so happened that an old pal of mine, Franny who was aged 17, was in Polmont when I arrived. He was a quiet lad on the outside but a good friend who showed me that his loyalty was just as strong inside as we had with all the guys from the Temple area.

As I walked into the recreation area Franny came to me and handed me a sock and said, "Fill it up with the snooker balls," just as four older guys entered the snooker room.

After a couple of minutes of intense talk with our intended foes, the matter was defused and the snooker balls returned to the table where they belonged. Franny and I left the snooker room in peace with no tension or recrimination.

I actually became pals with a couple of these guys, even if it was only for the few months I was in Polmont, but my cousin was still my main ally.

I was then transferred to Noranside, in Forfar, which was an open borstal. It was here my sewing machine skills came in handy when I was taken out of my farmyard duties. These farm duties, or should I say duty, was to stand on top of a large flat topped pyramid of dung with another inmate and a large pitch-fork. Our instructions were simple – keep shovelling the contents that we stood on into a trailer that just came back and forth all day. One good thing about this job was that I slept like a log and it helped put a few of my muscles into shape.

Being placed into the textiles work shed that made prison shirts released me from the empty field that housed the dung pyramid. It was a new placement that I was happy to accept. In the textile department, where there were six of us, our quota was to make five prison shirts a day which paid us a full prison wage. This was financial luxury, for in comparison to this, I would have needed to spread dung over the whole east coast of Scotland to earn the same income.

A couple of things that stick out in my mind at this time were that I intended to do a comedy play with big "Woolfy" from the "Spur", another Glasgow gang, and a few of our other mates. We had planned it for a Christmas show for the inmates. Unfortunately (it depends on how you look at it) I had hurt my ankle badly while playing football so the play was cancelled as I was the organiser. I was disappointed that the rest of the inmates did not seem too bothered whether the play was on or not.

The other thing was that one of the guys had a Charles Atlas book regarding "Dynamic Tension" and how to look like a Greek god if you followed his instructions (and paid the money). After religiously reading the borrowed manuscript I abandoned it to do daily press ups, which I kept up for years ever since my meeting with Charles Atlas.

I could have given Charles a better piece of advice regarding "bodybuilding." All he would need to do was send his clients to do a week's shift shovelling the dung pyramid at Noranside Borstal.

Release and away to sea

I was released from Noranside early in 1967 determined never to go back behind bars again.

I had spoken to Mr Irvine (yes, he was still my probation officer) and as I said earlier he arranged a trial trip for me with the Woods Trawler Company in Aberdeen. While awaiting the result of this application I got a job in Glasgow with Lawrence of Partick, who sold household furniture. Delivering furniture was an employment I enjoyed immensely.

Some months later I got the letter offering me a two week trial trip with Mr Irvine's contact at the Wood's fishing company. I was excited about this but remember the train journey up to Aberdeen as being lonely.

My dad's pal, big Fids who was a Partick Thistle supporter and took me to my first football game when I was about six, was now living in Aberdeen, so I spent the night at his home before reporting to the ship owners' office the next day. I was then put into the *Seaman's Mission* for the night. The room I slept in was very clean and tidy, probably too clean and tidy for me to enjoy, as it was "too establishment" and resembled an upmarket cell.

The next day I got aboard our ship and was designated a bunk in the claustrophobic cabin below deck. This was an amazing experience for me, and, but for a rule's technicality, my life may have taken a different road.

We set sail and were well on our way when we had to turn back to Thurso to pick up a replacement piece of radar equipment that had failed on the trawler. We were met at the harbour during the night and without stopping, the package was thrown aboard as we turned and made our way out of Thurso's harbour. Our ship then headed North West for thirty six hours before we dropped our nets in the fishing grounds our captain knew well.

From the first time those nets hit the water it was intended that they would be emptied and returned to the sea every two hours. What this meant is that the nets were brought on deck, the catch emptied onto the deck, the nets checked and repaired when necessary, then secured and returned back into the water.

The fishermen then had two hours to gut the catch that was now on board and get the fish down into the hold before the next catch was brought up from the sea. Once the "gutting" was finished the men would be off duty.

An average catch would give a decent break between loads but a large catch meant we would just be finished one load and the next load was being trawled in to be dropped on deck.

So in essence, if there were big catches, you could work around the clock without a break – and on occasion we did. As a "trial tripper" I was only expected to do a normal shift which meant I could sleep all night if I wanted to.

This trip was hard going but I loved every minute of it. I did every duty and even when the men were on their break and in their bunks I used to sneak the captain a coffee as I loved the workings and controls in the wheelhouse cabin.

The captain was a hardworking man of few words, but with a continuous flow of coffee he would explain and go into all the things a trawler man should know. He even gave me the wheel for a while as he napped beside me. There was nothing to bump into so it was quite an easy task.

Four days before we were due home we managed to pull in catch after catch of dog fish; this catch is a delight to any sea going fisherman as the dog fish does not need gutted. This meant a short time working on deck between catches.

Needless to say we had a full quota in the hold so we left our fishing ground two days early to go home.

On the way back to Aberdeen I was on the roof of the main cabin sunbathing when a whale, nearly the size of our boat, swam alongside us for a few minutes. It was an amazing experience.

A wee funny side to this voyage was when one of the senior men, who had good patter, was seasick. Apparently he was seasick every trip he went on. Now you would think it would be just plain sea sickness, not at all for this wee guy.

When we left Aberdeen harbour to go to sea he was in charge of the nets. He would haul them out and spread them on deck to inspect for any damage. When it came to using the seal skin to tie at the end of the nets (this is strong and pliable when wet) he would be violently sick. The crew roared with laughter as he retched like a fog horn, threw the contents of his stomach over the side, wiped his mouth and continued with the seal skin part of the net to once again repeat his retching format. This happened every time he went to sea and the men still found it funny even though they had witnessed it for years.

Well this same wee guy who worked through some really tough weather, like the rest of us, without as much as a hiccup, had another laugh for us. When we were approaching land and he sighted it, even if the water was as smooth as glass, he would go through the same ritual of retching and being sick all over again. Even the guys in their bunks below deck knew that land was on the horizon with each retch that came from their colleague. Being sea sick when you spotted land was as unique as he was.

I took my sealed envelope with the written progress report prepared by the captain and thanked him for all his help and input. He wished me all the best and said I could make it, or words to that effect.

73

As a trial tripper I was not due any wages until I had been accepted officially as a deck hand, but the men I sailed with told me to meet them in the local pub the next day, Friday, once they had been paid. They would honour the old tradition of having a whip round for the trial tripper. I then went back to the Seaman's Mission and reported to the manager who had booked me in for the night as he took my sealed report card from me.

Next morning I was up bright and breezy, ready to go and looking forward to getting home, but first I had to wait on the Woods Company manager officer to see if I had a future as a trawler man.

"It's a really good report Pat," said the manager as he put my reference letter back into its envelope. "It's so good we are going to offer you a position in our company as a deckhand."

"That's great, my Ma and everyone will be delighted," I thought with a feeling of completion.

"When do I start?" I asked with a big grin on my face.

"It will be Monday, morning," he said looking through has papers. "Aye Monday," he repeated when he found his placement sheet. "You have to report to the college and you will be there for two weeks. You will keep your room at the Mission, during this period."

Well that would be okay I thought, as this was Friday I could still go back to Glasgow that afternoon and be back for Monday morning for the college.

Then the manager informed me that I could not go home for the weekend and that I was expected to stay at the Seaman's Mission for the next two weeks while I attended their college. I was bitterly disappointed.

I asked if I was due any money and was told that I would get paid the following week, once I had started the training at their college. If I did not stay for the training then, by their rules, no payment was due.

The manager was really apologetic but said that his hands were tied. He tried to encourage me to stay and was very friendly. I reluctantly told him I would get back to him and let him know. I headed for the pub and the shipmates who were well on the way to being drunk.

The official "chip in" was carried out, although only half the men were there by this time, but it was enough to get me home by train with a couple of pounds on top.

The trawler men asked what I was going to do, and it was easy to say that I was going home because I now had the fare. I missed my family too much – much more than a job could satisfy. So I went back to the Seaman's Mission manager and told him of my decision. He was as disappointed as me but reiterated that if he had the authority he would have let me home for the weekend, but those were the rules.

So through a technicality I walked away from a job that would have seen my life go in a very different direction. I was not to be a fisherman of fish.

Home again - 1968

At a party in one of our pal's houses that I was invited to attend, another pal, and future brother-in-law, was also present. An argument broke out with my future relative and guys from another district who were at the party. I took my pal's side and intervened but was then arrested and charged with assault and breach of the peace before being released on bail pending trial. The reason I write this is to explain that for years I always seemed to have a court case pending – from my youngest years and up into adulthood. So by the time my next misdemeanour raised its head I already had the worry of a court appearance over my head, which brings me to my next escapade.

6

I See The Bad Moon A-Rising

***Creedence Clearwater Revival* vs Matthew 24**

It was a warm night as we left the pub after the last bell had sounded. I had had a couple of pints of beer along with my five pals and we were in jocular mode as we took our usual position at the corner of Tambowie Street, with jokes and patter flowing freely.

At our corner stance we had a good view up Tambowie Street and the corner of Boclair Street which ran parallel with one another. From where we stood a small park separated the end of both streets from the main road, Fulton Street. So from our vantage point we could see all around. Life was good as we talked and laughed about old victories and losses, in our conquest of love (more bragging than anything else) and of war.

I don't think we were out of order as the two pubs in our catchment area were vacated with shouts of "Time gentlemen please" echoing in the night air.

Small groups of drinkers were saying "goodnight" and "cheerio" as they began to make their way home, some more unsteady than others, and some having a wee song to themselves. The atmosphere is what I loved, and still do, about the district of Temple. It was a close knit community and everybody was unique in their own special way as such districts are.

Our wee pal "Hocky" made sure that most residents of Tambowie had a nick name with a story to match. He gave people names that just made you laugh.

We had characters like "Boaby the Biter" who lived in the next close to me. Boaby and one of our other neighbours, Big Joe Donachie, were having a verbal dispute that spilled into a struggle – a struggle that saw Boaby bite big Joe. Now that is bad enough, but Boaby only had the one front tooth and that tooth was not in the best condition as he tried to gnaw at Joe's arm, hence the nickname; Boaby the Biter.

Others, like Doctor Surge, Lilly the Pink, Piston Feet, The Bug and Peanuts Rush, are but a few who were christened by our pal Hocky.

So there we were (Hocky too) as the pub crowd dispersed, and I would love to say we were innocent, but in reality we were singing the old song *I See The Bad Moon A-Rising* in between the laughter and jokes.

In essence we were probably too loud as we stood at the corner and perhaps needed moved on. Our night changed dramatically when the police van, one of those small Morris Minor vans, came speeding right up to the corner where we stood.

Screeching to a halt the police van doors swung open at the same time as the echoing cry of "Polis" resounded in our heads. This cry caused the usual Temple response to stampede, innocent or guilty.

It was like a herd of wildebeest spotting a pack of lions too late – it was that type of fright, and if there were medals to be awarded for "Best Starts" then it would have been a dead heat between the five of us as we looked for an escape route.

Davy, one of our quieter pals, ran towards Boclair Street where he lived, speeding along with another one of our mates.

Bosco, Hocky and I ran as though to follow them, but we turned up the small incline in the park and stood at the bus shelter on Fulton Street that looked down into Boclair Street.

This meant that the police could not follow us by van which they had returned to, but they managed to capture Davy as he slowed down outside his home. He was easily caught but he was protesting that he had done nothing wrong.

A skirmish started between the two policemen and wee Davy when the police officer brought out his baton and proceeded to direct Davy into the van with blows from his truncheon.

I looked at Bosco and he looked at me and without words we decided instantly that we could not allow this unprovoked attack to happen to our mate. Our own safety and liberty did not come into it; neither did the fact that we would be committing a serious Breach of the Peace to say the least. So in essence we left common sense and wisdom chained up and impudent against the consequences. Even the thought of going to prison never entered our minds as we went to help our pal.

We managed to get Davy free from the arresting officers but the elation of that was the knowledge that there would be consequences to pay, and pay we did. The two officers had abandoned their van, and one of their hats, as they ran up Boclair Street and out of sight after we confronted them.

I managed to corral the five of us up into my Ma's house. Locking the front door I turned out all the lights and closed all the room doors, and no sooner had we managed to get the house looking unoccupied and quiet than we heard the police cars and vans roar into our street. Not a soul was on the streets of Tambowie that night but every curtain twitched in expectation at the unfolding of events.

It was like an invasion as we heard police car upon police car outside my bedroom.

It felt as if the full force of Glasgow's men in blue had turned out, certainly enough men with them to guard the whole of Knightswood. I don't know how many police officers came up the stairs but they banged on my Ma's door without mercy.

Silence, as no one dared to breathe, before another bang, bang, bang, was violently rapped out on the door knocker.

The letter box opened, and we could hear whispering. A couple of minutes passed and then the sound of feet running back down the stairs, then silence.

I managed to make a "shhh" sound as we all lay on my bedroom floor for an age as we listened to police cars patrol up and down the street. We knew we were in trouble, serious trouble. The reality of what we had done was coming home to roost. I was already out on bail for assault, so my mind was made up before we left my Ma's house early that morning as the five of us split up to go our own way. I was off to England along with Bosco; that was the only option I had left and since Bosco agreed with me, then it was a done deal. The following day Bosco and I got on a train and headed to Nottingham.

We both had left instructions with one of Bosco's relatives for our wages (we were both employed) to be collected from our employers and be brought to us at the address we would forward when we got a flat in Nottingham.

Within three weeks of our confrontation with the police in Temple we had left the Nottingham flat and went on to secure a rented flat in Lewisham, London. We both worked in a lemonade factory on the Old Kent Road, but the desire to get home was strong.

We met up with Tam, a friend of Bosco's, who lived with his mum and family and we spent some sleep over nights at their house.

Tam, who was a quiet lad but not to be messed with, went around with another good lad who was just as quiet as the four of us socialised.

We managed to stay in London for a few months before we called it a day and headed back to Glasgow.

In trouble – again

I could miss out this part of the story, but as I was writing the realisation of what type of young man I could be came strongly to my mind. Twice during our stay in London we were involved in fights. One of these fights was in a pub that ended up with Bosco and I being chased by two burly bouncers after we had sorted out a difference of opinion with some regulars of the local hostelry.

The second one was more serious. We had been involved with some heavy local youths after a Saturday night fracas and they must have felt that they had come off second best.

The next morning at breakfast I was having a cup of tea, Bosco was pressing a shirt in the hallway and while Tam was away for a newspaper his pal was putting away the dishes.

We heard a car screech to a halt outside the front door as I heard Tam's ma shouting, "They have got my Tam."

I instantly ran for the front door, passing Bosco's ironing table, and lifted the first garden tool in the hallway (the garden was directly outside the front door). An old black car was stationed on the main road empty, with all four doors open. Wee Tam was being set upon by the cars four occupants just as I got to the gate. Their act of retaliation on wee Tam stopped as I lifted up the garden implement. It was then I noticed that I had picked up a pitch fork, I let out a shout just as I heard Bosco behind me.

We ran towards the assailants as the group of four began to break away. Bosco was at my side within seconds before I saw that he had pulled the hot iron from the wall and was going to use it for protection. Between the two of us we held our ground as the four guys made their way up the street.

By the time we were walking back to the house a small crowd had gathered. My mind was racing; this was twice that the locals had come off second best.

"What do we do now?" I thought as a bruised and battered Tam was being attended to by his friend and his mum.

"Right everyone, into the car," I heard myself shout. "Right now, they will be back with handers," I continued.

So within a couple of minutes we had chased this gang and now we were driving their car up and along the Old Kent Road. So our stay in London came to an end.

The next couple of days we managed to lie low in our own flat before we could collect our wages from the lemonade factory where we were working.

We kept the car and I drove the four of us back to Nottingham as I was the only one who could drive. The old car was then abandoned in one of Nottingham's main streets.

The next day Bosco and I separated from Tam and his mate (who both headed back to London) and we made our way by train back to Glasgow. So I suppose telling a story, we can tend to leave the grotty bits out, and I have, but I feel that I should record these incidents because I would never claim that I was a goody two shoes. But in my heart I always battled with myself at the wrong things I was doing, my conscience never allowed me the freedom of feeling justified for anything I did wrong, yet I continued to do what I did not want to do and could not manage to do what I really wanted to do.

By the time we did arrived back in Glasgow two of our accomplices in the police car rescue had been arrested and sentenced to imprisonment for their part in the melee.

The third accused had been arrested at a later date and he too went to trial and was sentenced to prison after being found guilty.

I felt condemnation for it was only Bosco and I who had really participated in the release of Davy and yet the three of them received heavy sentences from six months to two years.

An honest self-assessment

I think we all (certainly from my background) have this idea about ourselves that make us think, "Ach, I wasn't that bad of a guy." But when we do an honest self-assessment on ourselves it needs to be said that I am ashamed of the behaviour over this period. I was probably looked up to for these incidents just as I had looked up to my peers when I was younger. I had looked up to them for this way of life that I was now leading, and I probably enjoyed it outwardly but never inwardly.

The thing about it was that after every violent event I would always think "I don't need to do this again, I don't want to do it again, I have proved myself." Approved myself from what?

While still on the run I went to live with my wee auntie Ann in Govan and got a job as a bus conductor with Glasgow Corporation and was stationed at Ibrox garage. During this time I visited my family every weekend. It was on one of these visits that I was almost captured.

I was walking down Tambowie Street and was almost at the "corner" (the same crime scene as the police van incident) when a police car came skidding around the corner of Fulton Street and headed straight towards me.

I turned and ran into the nearest close and into the back court, which was a few yards from where I was walking. It was the same close where I had attended the party.

As I vaulted the railing with one leap I ran to the left instead of going straight up and through all the back courts. I emerged from the adjacent close seconds later, hoping the squad car had made its way well up into Tambowie Street, and that they did.

"Déjà vu" came to mind as I ran up the grass incline, where Bosco and I had stood before our folly took place, and over Fulton Street to make good my escape. Apparently police stopped the local bus and searched for me after they had checked out the back courts of our area – but to no avail. I got back to my aunt's house without any more confrontation and made my early shift as a bus conductor the following morning.

Summer came and I had no peace whatsoever, I think it was more the guilt of my pals getting jail and me being free. Looking over my shoulder every minute of the day did not help and I had considered giving myself up.

Summing all things up I knew that I would get a heavy sentence – there were other outstanding charges I was still to face – but the chances of physical retaliation from the police was now not a concern as time had passed.

On the move again

Within a few months I was on the move again. I put my notice in with Glasgow City Transport and bought an old 1957 MG Magnate for £30. The car needed a wee bit of repair work but this vehicle was to take me back to London (talk about a dog going back to its vomit), or so I thought.

After collecting my wages from the bus depot and my car from the house of a part time mechanic (well that is what he called himself), I picked up a fellow bus conductor who wanted a lift to London and off we set for the big smoke.

I changed our destination as soon as we were on the road. For some apparent reason I decided to do a detour and head for York. At the back of my mind a thought became active, "Go and see your granny." I had only met her once as a child, and only my Ma from among her family had shown any time for her.

She had apparently abandoned her six children to an orphanage and left them in the care of a convent. My Ma had been down to England a couple of times to visit her and even bought gifts back for us. It seemed that it was only my Ma had forgiven her for whatever reason she left her family.

So there I was, chapping the front door of a granny who probably could not even recognise me, but I was hopeful when she opened the door that she would.

She realised I was "Betty's boy" straight away and seemed pleased to see me, but she was more relieved that we were passing through. She spoke to her partner and we were invited to stay the night. Her partner even took us down to his social club that night and I got on just fine with him. I never saw her again but I'm glad I paid her a visit.

First thing next morning we left York and got onto the M1 motorway. After travelling for a while, smoke started to come from the exhaust and thoughts of my part time mechanic flashed through my mind. A wee blue light brought my fugitive status to an abrupt halt as the police car flagged me down.

It sounds a bit strange but as I was giving my name and address to the traffic cop I felt a release even though I knew it was payback time.

"There's a warrant out for your arrest, Mr Clark," said the courteous officer, after he radioed in my particulars.

"Aye, I know officer," I said with a surreal sense of relief and a feeling of "that's it – finished."

So my bus conductor pal and I were taken to Newark Police Office (near Nottingham, yes I know!) where he was allowed to go and make his own way to London.

I was asked what I wanted to do with the car as it would now be towed into a local garage. I informed the surprised officer that I did not want the car, nor did I have the money to have it towed away, neither did I have the desire to have it collected at some future date.

I was tempted to give my mechanic's address in Glasgow and tell them to get him to pick it up, but I don't think he would have been amused at my retaliation. So a note was written up by the sergeant for me to sign the car over to the garage that would tow it off the road, allowing them to keep the car to offset any financial charges.

Being arrested was a huge weight off my back which seems strange as I had freedom, money, a car and a vision of moving on to better things. But in essence I was in chains to my conscience by being a fugitive; at least in prison you get a liberation date, but on the run all you have is the expectation of a pending sentence. No peace can break through wrongdoing.

A special 'fish supper'

I had spent Sunday and Monday in the cells at Newark Police Office when two burly Glasgow CID officers came to collect me. They let me know who was boss but in a professional manner, much to my surprise, however, there were no threats or retaliation considering my actions against their colleagues.

"Where is your own car?" I asked the big Glasgow cop as we left the police station in a marked squad car with its English driver. "We are flying back to Glasgow," came the reply from the taller officer as he checked my handcuffs were secured.

It's strange, but within an hour or so I was on friendly terms with my big guard. If truth be told, he was a decent and respectable human being, not because he did not say anything about my pending charges, but more like he just seemed to care and wanted to encourage me to toe the line, after I had told him that

I was fed up with running from the police and that I just wanted to get back and do my time.

Before we boarded the plane I was issued with a serious warning about my future health's stability – that if I did anything funny there would be physical consequences. He then removed my handcuffs just before we boarded the plane.

When we landed at Glasgow airport another police car picked the three of us up and transported us to the old Maryhill Police Station on Gairbraid Avenue, Glasgow. I was charged by the desk sergeant with breach of the peace, police assault and aiding and abetting a prisoner to escape. After these formalities were carried out I was taken to my cell.

I was to be held there for a couple of days but the tall officer who had never left my side from Newark, whispered to me as he was locking me up, "I will try and get you through to court quicker." As he left I heard him say to the desk sergeant, "He needs something to eat, it's been a long day."

About a half an hour passed and my cell door opened, "Here Pat, I got you a fish supper," said my big *"flying polis pal"* with a smile on his face. "Enjoy it and all the best. I will try and get your case heard as soon as I can," were his parting words as he locked my cell door never to be seen again.

Now you may find it strange but I felt he had become a mate even if we were not in the same team. But let me tell you what was stranger by far – getting a fish supper from a big polis man. It's totally unheard of that such a luxury was delivered to me by a senior officer of the constabulary. Other than that, it could have been a plain clothed angel, for it was the best fish supper I had ever tasted. Goodness, if any of my mates knew about the fish supper they would be raising more than their eyebrows.

When I appeared at court the following day, and after I pleaded guilty to the original (pending) party assaults charge, I was put on remand, waiting for background reports, at Longregend Remand Home. I was surprised that it was the only charge that was brought up and that the more one charge of assisting a prisoner to escape from police custody had not been used. But the assault charge was only a holding charge.

I must have been under the delusion that the courts had forgotten about my participation in the release of Davy from police custody, which was something that did not happen. Anyway, when I re-appeared in court weeks later, I was sentenced to two nine month sentences, to run concurrently, in the Young Offenders, E-Hall Barlinnie, for the less serious party assaults charge.

Confused? So was I. What had happened to the "aiding and abetting a prisoner to escape" charge? This would come back to unsettle me at a later date.

I was shaking my head and saying the same old thing as I walked from the courtroom to begin my sentence, "Never again." That was my mantra – that was my response.

As for the more serious charges I thought it would be a case of me being *"turned at the gate"*; to be held in reception and taken back down to court on my liberation date. That's what usually happened with any outstanding charges.

Not only was I confused, so too were the authorities who replicated my confusion when my name was called out for release from E-Hall on December 1970. I was not stopped at the gate, neither was I arrested outside the prison doors, so off I went home, happy as Larry. It was not something I was going to dispute with prison officers or wardens alike. I just accepted my good fortune and went home a free man.

I think I was allowing my mind the luxury of working out a scenario that sounded plausible to myself, and I came up with the thought that the Crown had spent enough time and money on two trials, and had given out heavy custodial sentences to three men, why should they be bothered with me? Wrong.

I was free for one day before I was challenged by an old police officer who was not liked in our area. I was rearrested and taken back up to Bar-L without any fuss or aggravation.

Although I was embarrassed at returning to Bar-L so soon; and even though I knew my release scenario was shot to pieces, it gave me no comfort to know that it was the authorities that had made the mistake. It turned out that the charges (of assault and assisting an escape) that I should have been taken to court for, before or on the day I was released, were not picked up on by the police or prison authorities. It was an older local cop who sorted that one out for the Crown when he arrested me.

That wee mix up and hassle aside, I was now in a bit of a dilemma as I was taken back up to Barlinnie. It was only a few weeks to my twenty first birthday, and this would mean that I would be returned to Longregend Remand Home near Airdrie until my court appearance. The thought that came to my mind was, "Stuff it, if they can make a mistake, so can I." This same mistake would take place again many years later, much to my mental cost.

So as I was being re-registered at Bar-L's reception area, I made a mistake about my age (I said I was twenty one) and was put on remand and into C-Hall.

This was the same hall I had served time doing Borstal Training, instead of going to Longregend. Now I was in there due to a date of birth mix up, much to my delight. One each on confusion between the authorities and I.

The court had accepted my plea of guilty for breach of the peace and assisting a prisoner to escape as they did not want to go through another trial (so my lawyer said). I was given another two nine month sentences to run concurrent. In essence, once again, I was fortunate enough to serve only nine months imprisonment for these charges. (Only due to the fact that there had already been two court cases to convict my five pals, the main charges against me would be dropped if I pleaded guilty to lesser charges).

The sentence was back dated for a month which meant I was released in the spring of 1971.

7

Ireland

Sunshine, Dublin and the IRA: 1971

As I have stated, there is no feeling better than getting released from prison, and as I walked out the Bar-L doors that spring morning in 1971 I was as high as a kite.

I was probably in the best physical condition I have ever been in, and going home to my family just enveloped the wonderful feeling of freedom. I remember going into town to buy clothes and was amazed that I had dropped two sizes from my waist due to self-training and the Bar-L diet. I felt as if I was floating with contentment and invincibility (no drugs or drinking was involved) as I walked through the morning sun soaked streets of Glasgow.

Being twenty one years of age, life felt good, being released from prison made it even better, but being free from any future pending charges, the world was my oyster. I was clear and I was clean. This was all fine and dandy for something I knew would fade, for I was experienced enough to know how these honeymoon feelings would subside, but for the days ahead I was going to enjoy them to the full.

It can take up to three weeks, all depending on the circumstances, for the euphoria of freedom to come tumbling down and normality to set in, but I cared not a jot as I walked along Argyll Street with money in my pocket that would allow me to buy some new clothes.

Now what to do? Find some work? Get a flat? All the thoughts of my future left when I met big Liam.

Liam was a middle class, and he was big, businessman who ran about Temple. He had a large, flat bed milk truck and delivered milk to shops throughout Glasgow. Liam had a nice flat in the West End and he had a fancy for more than one of our local lassies. Because of these affections some of our young local lads had had a few run ins with him, due more to jealousy than anything else.

When he offered me the opportunity to work as his driver on his milk run (I did not even have a driving licence) I jumped at the chance. I received a good wage and was offered the spare room, rent free, in his flat, which I accepted. This gave the big man a bit of freedom and a lot of peace from the young team to pursue the loves of his life.

The flat was never empty and Liam and I became firm friends. There was nothing better for me when he gave me the keys of his bottle green V8 Rover and asked me to pick him up at certain times of the day. In essence I was Liam's employee and he felt more comfortable having me on board than he did working alone, especially doing early morning deliveries in his truck.

Liam was quite secretive in business but when he told me he was going to Ireland to try and set up a milk supply link with local farmers I accepted his invitation to join him. So although I would not be paid a salary all expenses were covered.

In the autumn of 71 we drove from Glasgow over to Dublin, via Belfast, in the V8 Rover and booked into the Royal Dublin Hotel on O'Connell Street. The first week was great as I was left to do my own thing while my employer went about his business. He had made appointments in an attempt to cost milk being imported to Glasgow, or so he said.

I knew on the second week that the deals Liam had been trying to do were stalling although he said nothing. By the time the third week had come and gone he said we would need to move out of the hotel as he could not afford it. I agreed with him to give it one more week to see if he could do some business before we moved out. I told him that I intended to stay on in Dublin no matter what happened with any future deals he would do.

The IRA…

During this time both of us used to go down to the end of O'Connell Street, at the River Liffey, and listen to old IRA men speaking about their struggle to unite Ireland. Coming from my catholic background and being an avid Celtic supporter it was easy for me to stand and listen to what was said. I had no problem with the Irish tricolour as it flew over my beloved Celtic, so wearing a wee tricolour badge was no problem to me, besides I had an Irish heritage.

We had been approached on a number of occasions by a small, slim built man around my age although he looked older, who wore black circular glasses that seemed to have plain glass. His eyes seemed as dark as coal and he had a dominant persona about him which was highlighted with his strong Northern Irish accent. He would inquire where we were from and would grill us in a friendly sort of way about what we thought about the Irish situation and was it our own car that we were driving.

We never suspected or gave him a thought even after his third approach to us at these gatherings. He seemed to want to befriend us as he would always finish off our conversation with an invitation to go for a pint. I was not much of a drinker and Liam was not into alcohol at all so we naturally declined each time.

His persistence paid off on what would be our last few days at the Royal Dublin Hotel. On accepting his invitation he continued to insist that we go to our hotel for the drink.

My first thought was that he did not believe that we were staying there, so I allowed Liam to persuade me to let him join us. On arriving at the hotel we were taken a wee bit aback when our new friend insisted that we go to our own room and order room service even though we were now at the hotel bar.

I felt uncomfortable and a tad angry but somehow Liam and I relented and went along with his suggestion after his insistence. The barman, who had been waiting for our order, did not take any offence when I said we would just be getting room service.

As we walked along the long, narrow corridor in silence to our room, I was troubled like I had never been troubled before in my life. It's now I know what this feeling was but at the time it was just like a heavy anxiety.

I walked at the front with Liam behind me and our unexpected guest brought up the rear. Just before we got to our room Liam and I passed a room with a double door when suddenly the two doors were violently pulled inward and two or three well-dressed men rushed forward and jumped on our unsuspecting visitor. At the same time another plain clothed man came rushing towards us, and pushed us both against the corridor wall.

Yet another one of their colleagues followed from the way we had come and joined in the melee. Every one of these men jumped on our unwelcome guest and a struggle ensued on the ground. Both Liam and I were held back with eyes wide open as we heard the claim of "Garda! Police!" being shouted.

Probably for the first time in my life I did not want to jump in and give the wee guy getting the jail a hand. I had had enough of releasing prisoners. I saw one of these plain clothed men, who were all armed, with a hand gun which he had taken from the floored man who was under all these bodies. Within a couple of minutes they had secured and handcuffed the wee guy, he was then lifted unceremoniously to his feet before being ushered down the corridor.

At the same time, Liam and I were quickly ushered towards our room by the highly excited officer who had halted us in our tracks along with another of his colleagues who seemed to appear from nowhere.

Once inside our room we were put against the wall and after some minutes we were joined by a senior officer. He was obviously a boss as our two arresting officers stepped back to make way for him.

The new well-dressed man stood uncomfortably close to us as he looked into both our eyes by moving his head slowly from side to side.

"You two get yourselves back to Glasgow, you don't know what you are getting into here, so get home," he said in a gentle Irish brogue that held an authority that was more like wisdom, but it was a command. It was neither a suggestion nor a recommendation, it was counsel from an experienced man who knew what he was talking about. He went on to inform us that we were lucky men and that they had got there just in time. He knew both our names and also knew that Liam's dad was in the navy, so he was pretty clued up in what he was saying. Then he left, with his two companions following in his trail.

We sat for ages not knowing what had gone on. We discussed the possibility that the wee guy was into drugs or other such scenarios that would have warranted such an arrest. We did feel it strange that our new found friend only wanted to know about our lives in Glasgow and he had taken a special interest to know what Liam's dad did in the navy.

I think we were just glad we had got rid of the wee guy even though I did not want anyone to go to jail. He was now out of sight and out of mind. We shrugged off this escapade as just one of those things, not for a second thinking we were in any serious danger.

A Divine escape from 'Mad Dog'

Over twenty years later, while I was volunteering for the *Maxie Richards Foundation* I told this story to a Dubliner who was also working for Maxie. His name was Fred Prendergast and he just shook his head and said, "Well Pat, the Lord must have been with you guys, for what you are telling me I am certain that the man who was arrested was Mad Dog McGlinchey."

History has shown that this man was known as an IRA member who was a suspect in a number of killings. So on reflection there we were, two Glasgow men going to pro-Irish meetings while driving a bottle green (army colour) car and staying in a posh Dublin hotel.

Did he think – if it was him – we were spies? Did Liam's dad being in the navy have any sway to his summing us up? Was the gun that was taken from him to be used on us? I didn't know at the time but I know now that I was being protected and that protection has followed me all the days of my life. Only through Christ do I now realise the seriousness and the protection of that situation.

Fallout

So getting back to the story, and writing about a few things that happened that week before and after we left the Royal Dublin Hotel.

At this time I was seeing a lovely English girl who worked in a restaurant. So all my spare time – when Liam was on business and she was not working – was spent with her, and as she was learning to drive I had Liam's permission to take her out for lessons (even though I still did not have a driving licence) and assured him that she would pay for the petrol.

One day, Liam decided to sell his car (he always said he was low on money) but apparently to do this we needed to go to Northern Ireland as it was not possible to sell a car registered in Britain in the south. I asked him if it was okay to invite my girl along, to which he agreed. The three of us travelled up from Dublin towards Belfast.

My big pal seemed to be agitated and short of conversation that morning as my girlfriend and I were in the back seat. He was not interested in any conversations that I tried to engage him in.

My young lady had fallen asleep on my shoulder when Liam suddenly pulled the car into the kerb in a village just before Belfast.

"That's it," he said, aggressively, turning right around on his seat to face me. "I don't have any more money left and we are too low on petrol to go any further. Ask your woman for money to get petrol. Now!" he demanded as his face grew red in front of me.

My big pal was not the type of man who wanted nor courted confrontation, so I was taken aback at this attitude and even more upset that he thought I would do such a thing by demanding money from this girl when it was his car we were going to sell.

"Give yourself a shake big man; you are on to plums if you think I am going to ask her, show a wee bit more respect," I retorted angrily as I prodded my finger into his red cheek.

What happened next was so out of character for my employer, as he took me by surprise when he got out the driver's door and opened the passenger door where I was sitting. I thought he wanted me to vacate the car.

I had no doubt that my girl had heard all of the conversation as her eyes opened just as Liam fell on top of me with his hands around my neck. Liam was a big man and I mean big in every sense. He managed to get a vice like hold around my throat as he replicated a giant redwood tree being felled at its base. I was now under his whole body weight and if I had not been able to get my arms free I doubt I would be writing this book. As the oxygen was being forcibly refused access to my lungs, I heard my girl scream as she opened the door and ran away up the street.

"I'm in a bit of trouble here," I thought as I put my hands on my attacker's face. I forced my two thumbs at each side of Liam's mouth and pulled with all my might, but to no avail. Liam's vice like grip was not easing in the slightest.

I was well on the way to passing out as I reached down and found an empty bottle of lemonade on the floor of the car. Somehow I found the strength and the space to deliver a blow to the big man's head.

He released me at the point of me becoming unconscious and as he drew backwards I lifted my two feet under his chest and shoved his bulk on to the road.

I remember that I wanted to smile as I saw his trousers were hanging low on his body, but with the oxygen I was gulping in, I was too busy trying to stay alive. I swallowed in the best air in the world and even though I was suffering with things popping in my eyes, I vacated the car before big Liam could get up and get his bearings.

I was forced to hold him off with a few blows as he tried to secure his trousers while at the same time trying to get another hold on me. I got him under control and the fight left him as he recognised that I now had the upper hand. Just at this moment two uniformed police officers appeared at the car and demanded to know what was going on.

In between gasps and trying to breathe I explained that we were actually pals and had had a disagreement but that the problem was now sorted out. No sooner had I said this than big Liam said, "I don't know this man, I was in the shop and when I came out I caught him trying to steal my car."

I felt like another pass out was coming on at this ridiculous explanation, and even though we had had a fight, the rules are you do not get the police involved; neither do you grass and even worse, you do not grass and lie at the same time to benefit yourself.

With no voice left to say anything, I just allowed myself to be arrested, without protesting, and taken to the police station for questioning. There were more important things than being arrested… like breathing and keeping my windpipe open. I was also more concerned about my girlfriend who had bolted just before the police arrived than what was to happen to me.

Liam and I were questioned separately and I stuck to my story of it being a mountain out of a mole hill. I didn't know what was going to happen as Liam was sticking to his story of me trying to steal his car.

The outcome was in a balance if I was to be charged with attempted car theft or not when one of the officers said, "Let me see your neck." I was wearing a shirt with a woollen jumper that had a zip at the neck.

Once I exposed my neck my jailer took a sharp intake of breath. My neck was swollen and even though it had only been an hour or so since we had been brought into the police station, Liam's finger marks were clear to see on my bruising skin. Both of us were read the riot act and warned that if we did anything at all out of the ordinary, our feet would not touch the ground. Liam went on to insist that he should leave first as he was heading for Belfast. I honestly did not care about my big associate as my destination was Dublin and the girl I had invited to join us for "a wee day out."

Liam was allowed to leave first as we were literally thrown out of that police office. Twenty minutes later I headed down the road towards Dublin. As I walked southward Liam passed me heading in the same direction without as much of a glance.

It took me hours to get back to the fair city as I walked a large part of the way but got a lift on my last lap. I went straight to my girlfriend's flat instead of the hotel and spent the night there. Early in the morning I left her flat feeling assured that she had accepted my apologies, but that was the end of that short relationship.

As I made my way back to the Royal Dublin Hotel from her flat I tried to console myself that it was because I was a bad driving instructor. On getting back I sat in our room and had a talk with Liam – he was beside himself asking for me to forgive him; it was totally out of character. It was no problem for me letting bygones be bygones, so I let him take me for a coffee.

Life in Dublin and another brush with the IRA

Still in Dublin I managed to get a job with K-Construction as a builder's labourer. I was on a job trawl when I asked this big guy on the building site if there were any vacancies available.

He stopped what he was doing, looked me up and down, and then asked softly in a broad Scottish accent, "Ur ye Scottish son?"

"Aye," I replied feeling all nationalistic.

"Well, we will make exceptions for you, start in the morning son," he said as he continued with what he was doing.

I managed to get a basement flat in Mount Pleasant Place in Ranelagh, Dublin, so that was me up and running and I returned the favour to Liam by allowing him to share my flat.

After a couple of weeks Liam too got a job on a farm, well that's what he told me and by the smell of him at night I did not disbelieve his word.

So things settled down for a few weeks as we both concentrated on our labours. We would take in the odd movie and also stop over at the GPO building to listen to the Nationalists (IRA) talking about independence.

At one of the last meetings we attended on O'Connell Street it was suggested to us that if we were interested in helping with the plight in the North then we should go to an office unit and see all the paraphernalia that they had.

The office was on the top floor at Lower Kevin Street, I think it was a shop entrance and the gathering was upstairs in the top flat. It was being held in a largish sized room in which all the walls were covered by newspaper cuttings and propaganda pamphlets and with tea and coffee available. It was just a 'get to know you' type of gathering with no agenda to speak of as we met a few of the men who had attended.

Being from Irish stock all this information rested easy on my mind and I decided to go to a further meeting to be held in a house as I wanted to be involved. I was given the address and told to be there at a certain time and I would meet a number of others waiting to attend. We were to stand behind a wall or hedge at the rear of a house and would be summoned in when it was our time to enter.

A few weeks passed and on the night of the meeting I found out that Liam was intending to go too; this did not rest easy with me. As two meetings were planned for that evening I decided to go to the later one, so I made an excuse as we were about to leave the flat and said I was not going. I knew Liam could be loose with his mouth so I did not want him to have any information about my intentions or involvement with this group of men.

Now I need to say that I had no intention of picking up guns but I thought I could be used by the organisation to get finance one way or the other; a stupid mind-set at the time, however, it was a cause I seemed to be drawn into. I wanted to help the Catholics of the North and the way they had been treated and by joining this organisation I could help. I most probably would have got up to my eyes in it but my God had another agenda.

As I stood in the darkness outside the rear of the house with several others, we watched the class of men who had been in the earlier meeting leave, (Liam included), before we filed in to take their places. Once inside we were spoken to by an articulate man a bit older than me. I can't remember anything he spoke of but he did finish by stating we would need to take an oath that we would be true and faithful to Ireland. This was done in Gaelic as we all repeated sentence for sentence our allegiance to the cause.

On leaving the meeting I felt as if I had perhaps got into something I might regret, but I had also felt closer to this organisation than before I entered.

We were informed that we would be contacted in due course. I did tell this guy that I could not do anything with them if Liam knew I was involved.

I was to find out months later that my mother's house had had a visitor asking about me. This visitor knew of my family from Maryhill.

A few weeks passed and I was working away with K-Construction while Liam did his bit on some farm. I did not see much of him as I started to socialise with some locals from work.

God works in mysterious ways, and he did this with me when he evicted me from Ireland within a few hours. As I said I was busy in my work and had become friends with one of the other labourers, Mick (I think he was a casual worker). We finished work on the Friday night and on our way home he told me he had no digs for the night as his mother had thrown him out. I immediately offered him my living room couch or floor, whichever he preferred. He was delighted, so when we got back to the flat I introduced him to Liam.

As I would be out working the next morning I suggested that Mick just hold on with Liam and we could go out when I got back from my shift. He agreed and was delighted just when Liam informed both of us that he too, for the first time, would be working overtime on the Saturday morning. Mick said he did not mind staying in alone till we got back.

After a good morning shift at K-Construction I returned home to Mount Pleasant Place to find that all my possessions were gone. None of the furniture was touched, but all my clothes and money had vanished.

The suitcases were away too but the flat was not even messed up, I could not understand what had happened, I just could not get my head around to thinking that I had been robbed. While in this state Liam appeared from his work. He checked over his belongings and his cash had gone too but his clothes (well I did say he was a big man) were all still in his wardrobe.

I think I got angrier in front of Liam than I would have if I had just been by myself. I allowed this anger to rise from deep within. "Right," I said to no one in particular, "let's go and get this guy."

Liam just nodded his head in agreement as I told him I would deal with this situation myself as we went from pub to pub looking for Mick.

After an hour or so the pressure of anger subsided as I began to think what I was going to do next. We went back to the flat without getting any information about our thief. I just reported that the flat had been broken into and left it at that. At least that would keep the landlord happy just in case my guest had done any other dastardly deeds to any of the other flats in the building.

I had about five pounds on me and still owned some clean underwear and socks along with a clean towel. In beside my five pounds was a dry cleaning ticket for my good suit, at least I had something to wear besides working clothes. So I went to the dry cleaners and paid for the suit before making my way back to the flat.

My mind was racing, "What am I going to do now?" I challenged myself as I went through the pockets of the cleaned suit. In the top pocket of the jacket I found about forty pounds neatly folded and flat due to the suit being cleaned and pressed. I had honestly forgotten I had put it there weeks prior.

I smiled and said to myself as clarity hit my mind like a breath of fresh air, "I am going home."

I can't remember the cost of the aeroplane flight but I had enough to get me home to Glasgow. I arrived back in Glasgow that very same night with only enough money to buy some chips for me and one of my mates.

No more contact was made to or from the group I had taken an oath with (I was later to renounce this oath when I became a Christian). I was never to see Mick or Liam again, nor to hold any ill feelings in the route the Lord allowed me to take.

The thing that I remember that cold night back in Glasgow was being free and back among my own. It was as if the whole Dublin thing had not happened. I had left my work in Dublin on the banks of the Liffey at noon, and that very same night I was in a Glasgow "chippy" buying chips. It was the end of a chapter, a chapter that would be opened years later when I understood God's hand was on me in more ways than one.

8

Bingo and the 'Big Hoos'

My Ma liked her bingo and was known to carry a few membership cards in her purse. She suggested that I try for the job vacancy in the Mecca Rosevale Bingo Hall as an usher.

"C'mon Ma, give me peace," I thought silently as she left to go to the bingo in question. It was once a picture hall now revamped that I frequented often as a youth.

Then I realised that there would be an army of women and that it would be a great laugh even though the wages were on average £12.50p per week. Besides, it was time to get back into employment as I had not worked since I had come back from Dublin a few weeks prior.

So I dropped in for an interview my Ma had arranged that same week and was given the job by a good manager called Harvey McManus. Harvey was a Geordie with a great sense of humour and it was a pleasure working for him.

On my first week, my duties were to watch the door and welcome in the customers before the bingo started. I was then to go on duty as an usher in the hall, checking bingo claims from excited customers who had won. As I looked at the caller I knew that was the job and the position I would prefer rather than being a steward.

Within six weeks I was promoted as the full time caller, a position I thoroughly enjoyed just as much as the increase in my wages, now £26 per week. New suits were ordered and my brown hair was streaked with wisps of blond (dyed). Just add a gold neck chain and you have a modern "walley."

I often laughed at myself at the thought that I thought I was "cool." Even to this day it still makes me smile.

Over a year later I went for an interview with *Top Rank Bingo* as a regional bingo caller. I got a position that only required sixteen hours labour per week. That meant eight shifts (at two hours a session) in the five Glasgow halls owned by Top Rank; all for the princely income of £70 per week. This suited me as I was on call for any emergency that would crop up at any hall that needed a caller.

At that time I decided to go into the retail fruit trade through some contacts I had and I took on a partner, John, to help me. After purchasing a van we would go to the fruit market early in the morning and stock up with boxes of fruit. We had a pitch in Kilmarnock that we would go to every morning to sell our merchandise.

Our stock had to be sold before twelve o'clock as I had to get back to Glasgow for some of my "Bingo Calling" afternoon shifts. So I was probably one of the best dressed street vendors in the trade.

For convenience, I always wore my work suits when I sold fruit, and it was quite amusing to see the response I got from customers – especially if I was wearing my brown velvet suit.

My partner would load up the boxes on the street with fruit and all I had to do was sell it and bag it before he took away the empties. Our prices were usually five pieces of fruit for ten pence, so when people heard my wee sales cry, *"There they are ladies and gents, lovely satsumas. Good for the teeth, good for the legs and cheaper than candy balls. We are selling at five for ten pence!"*

It brought a few smiles as well as sales and we made a good wage with this venture that enhanced my bingo salary.

Being the caller, I then met my future partner and wife, Margaret, who was the prize bingo manager in the Rosevale hall. Guess what? We ended up with a full house when our darling Tracy was born on February 23rd, 1973. I had my own flat and Margaret managed to get a house, after living with her relative, for both her and our daughter.

To the 'Big Hoos' (Barlinnie) again

One damp midweek night I went to a Celtic match at Parkhead with some mates and on the way home we decided to go for some fish and chips.

A bit of light banter was had with one of my pals, Jim, and two young opposing supporters whose team we had beaten that night. I was not involved at all and it was light hearted to say the least.

As the two young boys left the "chippy" they turned in tandem and shouted some profanity that made us all laugh. Jim ran after them in mock pursuit as we awaited our fish suppers. We then heard a commotion outside and went to see what was going on.

On exiting the chip shop we saw that two police officers were holding Jim by his wrists. Jim was protesting by saying, "It was only a laugh, just a bit of kidding on." We approached the officers and tried to explain what had happened, we even invited them in to speak to the shop owner, but to no avail.

I guess I should have left at this point but I was upset at the injustice of it. I was warned by the senior of the two officers, a sergeant, to get away but I continued with my vocal expression of the injustice that was taking place. I guess I was committing a breach of the peace by not taking the sergeant's good advice. All I can say about this is that I was then grabbed by my coat sleeve by the sergeant who had released Jim into full custody of his younger colleague and was pushed back against the wall

As he did this he rubbed the back of my hand against the rough-cast of the wall while facing my three remaining friends and telling them to go home. In one mad second I wrenched my hand from his grip and as he leaned towards me to restrain me I punched him full on the jaw.

"Oh no, not again," I thought in disgust with myself, as my four mates did a runner up Argyll Street. I was left face to face with the young constable as the sergeant lay still on the ground.

The junior officer had made it clear he did not want any more trouble when he let Jim go at the point when I had struck his colleague. And that was the same time I decided it was time for me to go too.

I was a bit surprised to see that the younger officer had taken the decision to pursue me as I tried to make my escape good. As I turned and ran around the first corner in the opposite direction that my mates had taken, I saw a police van coming towards me, so I decided to run past the first close and headed for the second close, intending to do my "get free quick trick," by going into the back court and emerging from the first close I had just passed.

Well, that was the intention but I never made it as I was arrested in the stair well of the first close I was supposed to exit from. I think I might have made a few noises of pain as I was arrested by two or three officers who were determined that I was not going to escape.

While lying on the back stairs of the close under a few officers I was handcuffed. My left arm was pulled out from under me and a handcuff was placed on my wrist which was on the ground. A booted heel came down on the top of the handcuff with full force and snapped it shut tightly around my wrist, per-haps to make sure it was closed properly.

Serious trouble

I knew I was in serious trouble when I was bundled into an un-marked police car that had pulled up beside the police van. I was unceremoniously thrown into the rear foot well of the car and two big plain clothes men jumped in with their feet on top of me. I will leave the rest to your imagination but when I finally staggered into the police station I pretended that I was stunned and nearing unconsciousness.

Standing at the bar and being charged I was made aware that it would be in my best interest to inform on my pals by supplying their names and addresses.

Things could get worse for me, so I said that the four guys with me were Chileans (there was an influx of Chileans refugees in Glasgow at the time) and a number of them worked in my dad's work in the Parks Department in Knightswood.

As I was being interviewed by different police officers, and knowing that by the time they went to check my story in the morning I would be on my way to court, I would not have to worry about any further physical discomfort being shown to me.

I was also aware that they would not be too pleased when the penny dropped and that my Chilean friends had never been to a Scottish game of football.

Being happy with my informant's story, I was then taken into the male toilet and handcuffed to the base of an old cast iron radiator. This was to hold me for a time as officers came and went. I shut my mind to any verbal stuff along with the odd kick which was nothing really, but the one who relieved himself on me was not a good aimer.

One of the officers who came into the toilet looked at my hand, which had become discoloured and seriously swollen, and decided I needed medical attention. The handcuff was removed from my swollen wrist and off I went to hospital in the early hours of the morning with two burly policemen in tow. My hand was badly swollen and completely numb but after my X-ray and examination I was told that no serious damage had been done, but had the handcuff been left much longer then it would have caused problems.

Now my dad, who had a good rapport with his Chilean workmates, wondered what was going on when they were accosted at 8am in the morning in the Parks Department bothy at Knightswood Park by CID officers.

My Da was not amused by my actions as his colleagues were questioned, but as most of them could not speak reasonable English, and they didn't even support Celtic, the police knew straight away what I had done. He was even more surprised when the officers took him aside and informed him that I would be appearing on petition that very day for serious assault on a police officer.

As I was driven to court I knew the drill and the consequences of my action. Even though it was one punch I was about to face a lengthy prison sentence. The legal system procedure was that I would be on petition which meant I would be remanded in custody for up to three weeks in Barlinnie's C Hall. During this time I would make an application for bail. That's what usually happens, although there could be special circumstances (it needed to be *very* special circumstances) for bail to be granted that same day.

As I was being ushered through the court that afternoon and into the judge's private room I passed my Da who was seated in the public gallery. We looked at one another for a second as I passed through.

"Da, it's me," I managed to say as I realised he did not recognise me. I later found out why when I viewed my swollen face and streaked hair which was stuck to my head with "pee" shampoo. The charges were read out before me and my appointed court lawyer.

"Police assault to severe injury, offensive weapon and Breach of the Peace," was said in the usual official methodical tone.

Offensive weapon? What offensive weapon?

"Offensive weapon… offensive weapon… what offensive weapon is this?" I thought as I turned to my lawyer about to turn the thought into a loud verbal protest. But my lawyer motioned me in such a way that I knew to be quiet. No plea or declaration was made and I was released on bail.

"Released on bail, you are joking?" I asked myself. "Just another one of these authority mess ups," was the thought as I was led away through the public gallery, past my Da, and back down to the cells to collect my personal property.

To my amazement the decision was right enough; I was released that very afternoon and hurried home with my dad in a taxi.

I so needed bathed and changed, I also needed to sit and think about what I had done and the serious consequences that would follow. But why on earth had I been granted bail? Was it anything to do with my physical condition? Or was there a report from my hospital visit available? Or perhaps when I went to Bar-L a medical report would be forced to include my physical appearance with the state of my hand, body and face? Why charge me with using a weapon and then not oppose bail, knowing that I had a previous conviction for carrying an offensive weapon?

From the second I threw that punch I was sorry I had done it. I really mean that. I had reacted in such a way that deserved punishment without leniency and I was aware that my actions had caused more than distress to the sergeant and his family. Surely they deserved an apology on top of my punishment.

All these thoughts and more circulated in my mind constantly up until my court case on April 5th, 1974, when I was sentenced to two, eighteen month prison sentences, to run concurrently.

Up until the trial I went into myself and prepared my mind for the long haul. I continued to work away as a bingo caller and kept my fruit business running. During this time I also passed my driving test (about time too). But the spectre of the trial was always there, as it was with every pending court case I faced.

I was encouraged by my lawyers to counter charge the police with assault and this I did but to no avail. I had no witnesses and the bruises on my body and hand were easily explained by the way I was arrested.

I will say I was kind of glad that I did not have to worry about proving how I had been mistreated and just dropped the whole matter when no evidence could be produced on my behalf.

My darling daughter Tracy was now just over a year old so I took the opportunity of visiting her more often than I usually did.

The weekend before the trial I put money on some horses, which was unusual for me, and won forty pounds. I bought a "wee cargo" of beers and stuff to add to the reservoir of alcohol that would be in transit to my Ma's house for my farewell party. I had kept my employers informed of my misdemeanour with plenty of notice that I was for the off, in fact I had told them from the beginning and they were content to see me continue with my work.

Misplaced friendship

I would like to add two wee stories into this period of waiting to go on trial, one is a story of misplaced friendship and the other is how truth always pays dividends.

You have already read about my exploits in Dublin, and by no means was I bigoted by any manner or means of the word. Yet, for me to consider anything about the Official IRA might seem to some to contradict what I have just written. But bigotry and religious differences and division was never a matter that was discussed in my home by either my parents or my siblings.

I was first made aware of the power and division that sectarianism causes with a simple personal experience.

I was in my early teens when a new lad, Jack, moved into our area from the East end of Glasgow.

We were amazed at this guy who was a couple of years older than me. He was a brilliant football player, a great fighter and had an amazing dry sense of wit that would flow at the appropriate time; I became close to Jack and he had my total friendship and loyalty, in fact I would probably have died for him, and I nearly did.

As I said, Temple was a close knit environment and friendship was a very high priority for us. So you can imagine my feelings during a lads' time together when the subject of friendship was mentioned and Jack was challenged to select who he liked the best in our group.

No contest I thought, as I was always with Jack and we did almost everything together – when I was not incarcerated that is – and while I was waiting on the nod of approval that would put such a silly question to rest, he picked one of our other wee pals.

This was a bit of a jolt to me. As a young boy I was hurt to the core, but went on to find out that he only picked the chosen one because he was a protestant.

It felt a bit strange that something so trivial could be so divisive and it demoted my feelings to a place where I thought that he believed I was not a genuine friend.

This instance did not stop my loyalty and camaraderie with Jack but being a Celtic supporter now had its drawbacks when pecking orders in friendship were being catalogued, something that I found alien.

Fast forward ten years for my second wee story and I was attending my "going away" party and helping to drink some of my forty pounds worth of beer and stuff when my front door opened and Jack came into my mother's house. He pulled me to one side and informed me there was a problem and asked could I help him out.

Apparently there were a couple of guys up from London looking for Jack and he needed to go to his sister's house where they had called and were supposedly searching for Jack. (His sister was married to Jim who in turn was in Bar-L along with a London firm incarcerated for the most serious of crimes).

Without any hesitation or thought for our own safety, one of our other mates, Wullie, joined us in the taxi that was ticking over at my close. I left my going away party when it was in full swing to go and assist a pal.

Leaving the detail aside, Jack encouraged both Wullie and I to run into his sister's house (carrying concealed weapons) to search for these Londoners while he stood outside with the two women who were the partners of the Londoners, and had been the cause of the disturbance at the house.

Goodness, I was going to face a Sheriff and jury in the next couple of days and there was I, up to my neck in potential violence once again.

By God's grace, only Jack's sister and the two women from London (who Jack then evicted from the flat) were causing the disturbance.

If the men mentioned had been there then I doubt very much if any of the three of us would be here today.

My trial before the Sheriff and jury was put back for a number of days and instead of being tried on a Monday it began on the Thursday and finished on the Friday when I was sentenced.

While in the prison van and on my way to start my sentence in Barlinnie we picked up some prisoners from the High Court. Jack's brother-in-law, Jim, came on board and when he saw me he managed to get a seat beside me. He was on trial with a number of guys from London.

I told him about the event that had taken place the previous Saturday in his house to which he replied in a hushed voice, "Keep that quiet Pat, you are lucky men. If the London boys had been there, then you would not be here."

It turned out that I became friendly with the main London guy who got the largest sentence of 30 years in Jim's trial. I didn't speak to Jack again for over ten years through this episode.

Once I became a Christian it was amazing to go and speak to my old pal who I had missed no matter what had happened.

We talk as if no incident had ever occurred, even me being second in line for his favour mattered not a jot.

The above incident has never been aired between us and unfortunately I didn't see him as much as I would have liked to, but I have changed that and we speak now and again.

I look at him as a dear friend who got caught up in something that was out of his control.

The power of an apology

Going back to the police assault charges I was to answer to, the charge of having an offensive weapon was serious and there was a chance I could be remitted to the high court for sentence – this would mean I could get a sentence starting from three years minimum imprisonment if found guilty. So I naturally pleaded not guilty to the offensive weapon charge and guilty to the police assault and breach of the peace.

To my lawyer's annoyance and surprise this plea was not accepted by the Crown, as they believed I had a case to answer. Because my plea had not been accepted I was put in the dock and my trial began after the jury was selected.

Witness after witness gave their version of the events before joining the public gallery that was directly behind me, when they had finished the case for the prosecution was over.

Now it was time for the defence, and I only had me. Just before I was about to give my testimony I turned around to the public benches directly behind, to see the police sergeant and his young colleague, who had both testified, sitting a few feet away.

It sounds a bit strange but I was not going to lose this opportunity no matter how it was going to work out and no matter if any of my pals could see me or not.

I looked straight into the sergeant's eyes and said, "I am really sorry for what I did to you; I hope you can forgive me."

A split second of hesitation passed as he returned my look and then, gathering his thoughts, he said, "Just turn round."

He looked embarrassed as he waved his arm slightly to motion me away. Now that may sound to you any way you want to hear it, but to my ears I picked up a softness that can only come from forgiveness.

Now allow me to get a bit spiritual here, because I don't know if the softness was in his voice, or if it was the softness that wipes away personal guilt, and no matter what, the only person that can wipe away guilt is the living God.

But hey, I was not a Christian at this time; I was a convicted criminal who had punched a senior police officer to his severe injury. All I know is that by the time I went into the witness box I was as free as a bird.

How was the court to know that taking an oath on the bible was quite a serious matter for me (thanks to my Catholic upbringing)? How were they to know my conscience was now clear and, more importantly, how was I to know that this weight that had been lifted was through forgiveness and not a prison sentence?

As we went through the trial I admitted everything during my stance in the witness box, much to the judge's surprise as he interrupted the procurator's cross examination to speak directly to me.

"Are you saying that you committed this assault on this officer? And are you admitting the breach of the peace, Mr Clark?"

"Sir," I replied, "I have never denied it. The only thing I do deny is the offensive weapon charge, I used no weapon. The procurator fiscal has been aware of this before the trial started."

The irate judge turned back to the procurator and spoke to him saying (in essence) "Does the Crown have any other evidence to stand up to what the accused is admitting to?"

Truth and honesty

With a bit of conversation the procurator agreed with the judge that the charge of offensive weapon should be dropped. The jury were then directed to find me guilty on two charges only. Because of honesty and truth, I felt I was shown favour from the judge when he sentenced me to a concurrent sentence rather than a consecutive one.

So instead of a referral to the high court for sentence, which would see me with a possible five years to serve, I was given two eighteen month sentences on both charges. That in itself was three years but the judge showed mercy when he declared the sentences to be concurrent. Above all, with having this trial, I got the chance to apologise to the officers I had assaulted.

Had there not been a trial then I could not have apologised, neither would I have known what a fool I had been. Just to think that entering my friend Jack's sister's house the previous week could have ended up more serious than the eighteen months imprisonment I received. But to top this off and on reflection, I can see it allows me to see that Father's hand was upon me, yet again.

There are a lot of things in life that we are disappointed or ashamed of, but remorse always comes after the fact or when wisdom kicks in.

I don't know how many times I would think, "Oh no, done it again," or "need to stop this," or "that's it, that's the last time," but I would always return to repetitious misdemeanours just like a dog returns to its vomit.

9

The Last Sentence

Sitting in the "dog box" – a three foot by six foot box room with a door and a wooden slat as a seat – at Barlinnie's reception area for over two hours, I was quiet as I thought through my life.

Being neat and tidy and having a few pounds in my pocket through two good jobs had not made tuppence worth of difference when I reacted the way I behaved at my latest arrest. It was time to stop, time to get off the bus, but I had said that time and time again.

Somehow this sentence was different, it felt different. Was realisation or my age finally kicking in? Or was it the apology I had given to a police sergeant who was a natural foe?

Off I went…back to A Hall and straight into the prison regime. As I made my bed and got my stuff sorted in my new freshly painted prison cell I remember looking up at the parallel prison bars on that lovely evening.

It wasn't the view that caught my attention, it was the song being played loud and clear from a fellow inmate's radio a couple of cells away. It was a song that had a wee effect in my heart and probably as near to a pity party as I have ever been. It was called *Seasons in the Sun*:

Goodbye to you, my trusted friend.
We've known each other since we're nine or ten.
Together we climbed hills or trees.
Learned of love and ABCs,
Skinned our hearts and skinned our knees.

Goodbye my friend, it's hard to die,
When all the birds are singing in the sky,
Now that the spring is in the air.
Pretty girls are everywhere.
When you see them I'll be there.

We had joy, we had fun, we had seasons in the sun.
But the hills that we climbed were just seasons out of time.

Goodbye, Papa, please pray for me,
I was the black sheep of the family.
You tried to teach me right from wrong.
Too much wine and too much song,
Wonder how I get along.

Among the thoughts that ran through my mind as the characters change from person to person in the song; it actually took my mind back to my first approved school and the night I prayed to the Lord to make time pass quickly. It was the time that home-sickness made me ill.

I was a bit disappointed with myself at being upset because when sent to prison I did not allow self-pity anywhere near my thoughts. But it was also a comfort to know that I could allow something to touch the soft part of my inner feelings that would rub up against my emotions and thus effect my conscience.

"I've had enough of this," I declared to myself, knowing it was a well-rehearsed statement, but like the professional offender I was, I meant it, just like I had meant it one hundred times before.

Keeping 'sew' busy

So I got through my sentence by working on mailbags, then as a sewing machinist in the laundry repairing prison uniforms, sheets etc. I was sent to work in the textiles department where we had a daily task of making three hundred pillow slips per day on our sewing machines. I was then moved onto making donkey jackets and then overalls. All these jobs had a target which had to be met before you were granted a full wage.

One day, I was taken aside with one of my fellow inmates and told that the prison was going to have a trial period of making products for the outside market. My mate and I were handed a few books with pictures and photographs of luggage and travel bags. The Principle Officer gave us the books then took us to the material store, just behind the sewing machines, to show us four very large rolls of PVC material, light brown, dark brown, black and a roll of black plastic which had a tartan design on it.

"Well get on with it," he said as he walked away with a nod towards the luggage books.

Both of us now had the best jobs in Barlinnie and we were probably more productive doing this work than we had been when we had the mundane tasks to perform.

We made suitcases and bags to our own design as well as copying designs from the glossy brochures. I just wonder if there would be any copyright issue as we produced replicas of branded luggage; but we cared not a jot, for we had a prison distraction of employment, and that was the bee's knees.

I actually went on a governor's request to see if it was possible to purchase a set of cases I had made. This request was refused but a few months after I was released I was delighted to see this same set of luggage on an afternoon TV programme which was discussing what prison authorities were trying to promote to help prisoners.

I loved this job and would do overtime not just with luggage but also with "wee earners" that would entail anything from making a child's Karate suit to spectacle cases as "homers".

I even made slippers for two of the London boys. They were now serving long sentences and so on security observation which meant that all their clothes were left outside their cells at night, including their shoes. The following morning the same two guys, along with their co-accused, were transferred because of a rumour that they intended to escape, so the slippers were never used.

One of the guys I was really friendly with did escape from a prison in England when a helicopter came down and picked him up from the exercise yard, I don't think he needed my slippers for that home leave!

You will have ascertained that I was always God minded – even when I was making a mess of it – and prayer got me through all my sentences...and life. Because of my Catholic background, however, that prayer regime meant that I was doing a deal with the spiritual falsehood of praying to the souls of the faithfully departed, along with the saints, so that they in turn could pray for me. I also got along by consoling myself that I could offer up any hardship as a penance, thus wiping out any "mince" I had been involved in.

This was my way of keeping on the right side of the road with the Lord. It was a total works strategy, trying to balance what was good and what was not so good, not knowing that *"For it is by grace you are saved and not through works that you should boast"* Ephesians 2:18.

I generally prayed by saying *"decades of the rosary"* and I doubt if anyone I knew said the rosary more than me. I probably

---

* At its most basic, the rosary consists of five 'decades' of Hail Marys (a decade means a group of ten), with each decade preceded by one Our Father and followed by one Glory Be to the Father.

said more decades of the rosary than was said in Lourdes or Fatima.

Saying these repetitious prayers over and over, like a mantra, I would seek peace for anything, from worrying about things in general, to frustration at not being able to sleep at night.

I guess I used this type of praying to keep my thoughts away from things that would frustrate or worry me, and things I had no say or influence over. Repetitious prayer, for me, was a comfort blanket.

Late one night in Barlinnie, with socks on so as not to disturb those inmates below, and silently reciting the rosary, I paced my cell unable to sleep and upset that morning would soon be upon me. Stopping in my tracks as I faced the metal restrained window, I looked up, and as I stared through the familiar bars I felt something stirring inside me.

"There's that bloomin' moon again," I thought as my mind caught a flashback to St Joseph's Approved School, but I then continued by speaking out quietly to no one in particular, when I said, "By the time I am thirty three I am going to have made it." This was my *Seasons In The Sun* moment for I was so sure, so certain of the words that flowed so easily from my mouth and from my spirit. I knew that these prophetic words were coming from deep within me.

I knew exactly what I was doing and saying. I was also very aware that Jesus had accomplished His mission by the time He was thirty three. What was good enough for the Lord was good enough for me. What I did not know was that my understanding of the situation, and the Lord's meaning of it, was set in two different plateaus. For in my interpretation I thought that by the time I was thirty three years old I would have made it, I would be at the top of the tree, financially free, set up, with all troubles laid aside, and I would be accomplished in life.

Silly me; as it turned out, I did make it. I was accomplished, I was freed and set up into a new life I never want to change. I became a Christian when I was thirty three but I don't intend to give you a sneak preview at this point so we will come to that part of the book in due course.

"Goodbye Papa It's Hard To Die" were the words of the song and that's what happened to me when I became thirty three, when "self" was rejected by a repentant spirit. What I will say is that the prophetic words I spoke out over myself happened; and it happened in a very special way.

Being released is as high as it gets on a mental mind-set, and the morning I walked free from Bar-L to be collected by friends was just as good as it gets. That same night I was awarded a home-coming party by family and friends. Life was suddenly good again.

My darling parents had bought me a car on my release. It was money they had saved hard for. I often wonder how they managed to put up with a son that caused them so much grief and worry, but I do know the favour of God and He did not miss me with an honest and loving Mum and Dad.

Another interview for the Bingo

When I got the message I was honoured and surprised as I was informed to go to the Mecca Bedford Bingo in the Gorbals to speak with their manageress regarding a caller's job.

Now this was not how I usually settled into freedom as I needed a couple of weeks to adjust and detox from prison regimes, but the opportunity was too good to miss.

When I met her she was so friendly and went on to say that she knew that I had been released from prison but was I available to start work as a bingo caller the following day. I accepted straight away, overwhelmed by her whole attitude to give me another chance with a firm I had worked with before.

After four weeks, however, I was struggling as I felt I had not taken the time out to get myself settled from the prison regime. It was probably just a mind-set but I knew I had to take a break to re-assess. I spoke to the manageress and explained that I would need to leave because my heart and mind were not focusing on the work. She graciously disagreed and said, "You are doing great, and I understand what you are saying. Let's do it this way, you take two weeks paid holiday and then come back and we will see how you are."

I was knocked sideways by her concern and I accepted her proposal and made arrangements to return in the two weeks.

On returning from my break I was met by a new manager who was not so accommodating or compassionate about an ex-con being given the position of a bingo caller.

I was led to believe that this may have been the reason why my manageress was replaced. So with the bit between my teeth at the reversal of my ex-manageress's compassion towards me, I said that it was Mecca who had asked me back and that I was now due compensation.

Yes, I know, but my wee statement worked and I was given a payment in lieu that suited me just fine. I never got the chance to thank my former boss for believing in me and giving me the chance to start again. A good woman she was, and the company paid me extra for her compassion.

So what to do next was my main thought as I drove away from the bingo hall.

Taxis – a new business

As soon as I heard *Boulevard Taxis* were looking for a driver to start I stood before the owner who gave me the keys to one of his cars and I was on the road. That first shift driving became a day with such a high and such a low in a short space of time.

There I was in my element driving people around Glasgow and getting paid for it – joy!

Later on in the shift I was called back to base to speak to the embarrassed owner who informed me that he would need to let me go because the original driver I had replaced had come back to him and asked for his job back.

"Sorry Pat, but the driver before you has been with me for years," was the reason he gave for my dismissal. I was so disappointed but managed to keep it together and asked, "What if I had my own car, would you take me back?" To my delight he made it clear that if that was the case then all I would need to pay him was the weekly "weigh in" rental by using my own car.

Now as I said, at that time my Ma and Da had bought me a car, a Mark 1 Cortina which I immediately sold (with their permission) before I purchased an old Austin Maxi from the Glasgow Motor auction. The following week I was a full time self-employed taxi driver who loved his job beyond belief.

I just wish that my old Austin Maxi had been as enthusiastic as I was. It had had so many breakdowns it was unbelievable, but that did not deter me. I worked hard and was rarely off the road when I went into my first hire purchase deal. I paid £400 for a Mark 3 Cortina from another taxi driver/car dealer with the promise not to miss a payment. I owned the car within three months.

I also changed my place of work to come under the *Red Line Taxi Company* in Clydebank where I spent a good and happy time. It was a job where I was free to visit my wee daughter Tracy, who lived with her mum, anytime.

I mention this episode in my life to say a few things that have given me insight into how things change so quickly.

I had saved up enough money to buy another car and it was a toss-up whether to put another private taxi on the road or buy an old Jaguar that had lain in my pal's garage for years. I chose the former as I knew a guy who had spent time in prison for culpable homicide. He had got into a fight and had thrown a punch from which a man fell and died. This man had a family and was keen to find employment. He worked for me until he found another job that he preferred.

Oh aye, the old Jaguar, its registration number was SC 777, ended up in the *Glasgow Transport Museum* and worth a pretty penny but my second taxi was more important to my new employee.

Just to round off this story with a wakeup call which happened in the early hours of a wet night when I was heading back to my flat after a long shift.

I picked up a young lady who wanted to go to Paisley Road West. Reluctantly I agreed even though I was tired. She then invited me into her flat as I waited for the fare to be paid.

She was gone for a few minutes before returning with the money. We sat and spoke and one thing led to another just as the door burst open and her boyfriend appeared with one of those large serrated kitchen knives. It had been a set up as I heard him say, "What are you doing? That's my bird."

I was stunned and very vulnerable as I moved slowly towards him with upheld hands. "I'm sorry mate," I said. "I was only dropping her off. Nothing happened."

He was so confident behind the knife he held – until I rushed to grab his wrist. Overpowering him I held on to his wrist that held the knife and with my other hand I forcibly grabbed the blade and bent it before taking it from him. Although I had cut my hand I just wanted to be free of the situation as my assailant sat quietly with his head bowed.

Now all I had to do was collect my clothes and get out of there. I had been set up and with temptation flooding through my being I had walked into a trap with eyes wide open not allowing my conscience to dictate my actions. Not only had it been a lesson but I was left with a cut across my palm and fingers just as a reminder

Haylyn Autos

Being around cars and mechanics during my taxi years I decided to move on and see if I could get into car sales and repairs with the thought of becoming a car dealer.

I had a pal who was an engineer and part time taxi driver but his heart was in cars and there wasn't anything he didn't know about them from electrical to paintwork – he was good.

Often, when you find someone who has talent like this they are at the fore of their skills but sometimes they lack ambition. Nick was the type of guy who preferred a pint to anything ambitious or adventurous.

It didn't take me long to persuade him that his talent could be used and his income increased by working for himself at something he loved doing. When I took him to see the small garage I had the chance of renting, he agreed to come in to a partnership with me and so *Haylyn Autos* was born

I just loved this wee building. It held three car parking spaces but there was only room to work on two cars at a time, but to me, it was like Arnold Clark's. Once we were up and running we would take in repairs as well as putting our advert in the paper to buy cars. *"A Baby Austin to an XJ6"* was the ad I placed in our newspapers as alphabetically this put us at the top of competing buyers.

Our garage was a great place to work until time had its way and flaws started to appear.

Nick had always been a man who enjoyed his drink but as time went on it became my job to go and get him out of his bed to go to work each morning. I don't think I regretted this for myself but I was angry for him that he could not shake the alcohol from his life.

First steps on a path to destruction

To my regret and shame, it was just before this time that I allowed myself to try marijuana and by the following year I had taken my first hit intravenously. Being a taxi driver I had all the time in the world to do what I liked but drugs were something that had never appealed to me. My wee pal who I thought the funniest man on the planet, Coots, used to hold court in his home most nights and I loved just to sit and listen to the patter and stories that ebbed and flowed from the company we kept. I would call a halt and go back to work in my taxi at the time they were falling asleep. Anyway, I was worn down by offers of taking drugs when I inhaled my first joint. I have never laughed so much in my life.

The laughter took me on and into a severe headache but the thing that came to mind was that this stuff must be better than alcohol and so a few of my pals (especially Nick) needed to convert to this way of life.

The following year I was in my partner Margaret's home watching our daughter, Tracy, as Margaret was out when I heard the door knock. I had just come out of the bath and had my house coat on as I opened the door. It was two of my mates that I smoked dope with. (It's really strange I did not understand what this chemical was doing, but I should have because even the name is a warning...dope).

"Okay Pat," was my mate's declaration as he faced me. "You said the next time we get 'stuff' that you would try it, well here we are. Are you ready?"

Now this was putting me in a spot and revealing my weakness of self-control as I had refused to take any intravenous hits in the past being content just smoking joints or taking speed although most of my close friends were using needles. Then I remembered that one night I had got fed up saying no, and had blurted out, "OK then, the next time you get stuff, I'm in."

So there I stood like a thirty bob dumpling with my arm held out to receive an injection of Diconal. My wee daughter was in bed playing with her toys.

Now let me be honest and tell you, when you hear about getting a RUSH with this procedure it is as it is described. Going from normality into oblivion as the syringe was emptied into my vein took a fraction of a second and was like a lift off that no speed of any air or nautical mileage can match.

"Whoosh." I had made it, I was there, this is what life is all about.

"How come I waited so long to try this?" were the thoughts that flooded my mind as I began to slide down the wall into a seating position of ecstasy.

Having paid for this experience my train of thought was shattered when I heard someone through the mist say, "That's you okay Pat, we are off."

"Oh no you are not, do you not know what just happened?" I slurred as they laughed at my attempt to tell them how lovely everything was and is.

They told me they had others to see and places to go (I think this must have been the first ever drugs delivery service in Glasgow). They vacated the house without another word from me and I was left alone. This serious abandonment only prompted me to get my wee daughter out of her bed so that I could talk to her until Margaret got home. It was the highest state of fulfilment I had ever felt with not a care in the world and speaking to my wee lassie who loved me more than anyone. But then as time would go on I would see it for what it was, and what it is, a deceiver, a divider and a killer without mercy. Its kiss of acceptance is a kiss of death.

My minute's experience of a touch from the Lord in 1982 allows me to judge and see that this drug induced episode was like dirt on the sole of your shoe compared to the purity and clarity of the Father's presence and touch, but we will come to that in due course.

Sammy's near brush with death

It was a bit strange because just the week prior to this my wee pal who had just injected me had almost been killed in a car crash. Our mutual friend Sammy, who bought a lot of cars from me, had purchased my TR7 for £1500 and I had made £500 profit with no outlay made. It was this deal that gave me the realisation that profit was not why I did what I did as he left with the log book and keys with our wee pal in tow.

One hour later while separating and looking at the £500 cash profit in my hand, I realised it meant nothing to me; money was not what I was after. As I was pondering this my wee pal came to the door in a bit of a state. I put the cash aside and let him in.

Before I could ask what had happened, he blurted out, "The TR7 is now a TR3 and a half. Sammy has just run it into a wall." Sammy had left me in my partner's house to go down to the boulevard and had ran the car into a brick wall on the way to Balloch. Both of them were shaken but fine and Sammy went on to sell the car for £300 scrap as he had not insured the vehicle.

When I asked my wee pal what he did when they crashed, he replied, "I just ran away, because I thought it was going to blow up." We would laugh at this for years to come.

Nick's side-line and a trip to Italy

Now Nick, who was in the garage with me, had a wee side-line when he came into possession of books of MOT certificates which he sold when needed. All of his income went on drink and I could see him slowly deteriorating at the time we were busted by the police.

I knew straight away what the police raid was all about and had to go through hours of interrogation denying I knew anything about the MOTs, while Nick was singing like a canary in the room adjacent to mine.

Many hours later, as I was expecting to be returned to Bar-L, a CID officer came and told me that if anything happened to Nick he would come for me personally.

When Nick and I were released from the police station late that afternoon, all I had for my pal was sympathy – genuine compassion – as I knew the grilling he must have had from the CID. I also knew that his testimony would not have much sway in court against the supplier of the fake MOTs.

It was then I decided that I would just hand the garage over to Nick (he was a really good guy) but told him that I would let our mutual friend know that he had spilled the beans on the MOTs source assuring him that I would not allow any retaliation.

As it turned out our mutual friend, Billy, had already been under observation by the CID but there was never enough evidence to charge or convict him. So, when I got a call from Billy saying he was getting away from it all, he asked if I would go to Italy with him as he was going to set up home there. He had relatives in Barga who had a café and he was determined to join them with his family and he then intended to open up a restaurant. The reason he wanted myself and a couple of other mates to accompany him was so we could all take turns in driving. Yes – drive all the way to Italy.

He was so determined to get away from Glasgow that he was putting all his belongings and household stuff into a hired van before setting off to travel through Europe to get to his in-laws. So there I was on my new adventure, driving the secondary car (a left hand drive Fiat bought from the Glasgow car market) that would accompany the box van truck.

It was a laugh and an adventure as we drove through Europe non-stop before we went through the Mont Blanc tunnel and into Italy before three of us returned with the hired van. One thing about this wee episode was that when we got to Barga we spent one of the days at the seaside. I was surprised no one else was in the water, not realising that the water there was heavily contaminated, hence no locals were bathing. This wee dip came back to bite me months later that year.

Not long after this trip my partner Margaret and daughter moved into my Temple flat as we set up home together. I kept the "Cars Wanted" advert alive and started trading from our house buying and selling cars.

As a young lad my passion had been playing football and that passion was fulfilled every time I went on to the football park as a goal keeper. All through my younger life Saturdays were for the great game I loved and for the game I played in. No fame or fortune (except I did get the *Player of the Year* award once), just an enjoyment that exceeded all my other passtimes and hobbies.

Having played for *Temple Star*, I then played for the opposition *Garscube* and enjoyed every kick and minute of this period, especially when a few of our *Temple* lads joined up with *Garscube*.

Anyway, I reported to the Smiddy Bar in Partick to get ready to go to our next game when one of my team mates said, "Pat, look at the colour of you," pointing to my face.

I looked in the bar mirror and, sure enough, there was a yellow tint showing clearly. Now I knew that the houses I used to frequent had the same colouring from the residents from time to time but it would always be dismissed as, "Just a wee bit of jaundice, man," explanation. "Not for me," I thought as I looked closer at my banana coloured eyes and straight up to the hospital I went.

After being admitted and tests I found out I had been infected with Hepatitis non-A non-B. At this time Hepatitis C was not fully recognised I presume.

I was kept in hospital for three weeks with my blood tested regularly. The doctors wanted to know about my visit and swim in Italy as they suspected that there may have been a link with contaminated water. I was happy that this is what they thought, not giving any thought or credence to my intravenous drug injections which I had in control (that's what we all thought).

A hospital visitor, a life changing gift, a voice

Just to interject, at this time in hospital I had visitors aplenty but one day, Davy came in to see me. He was another close friend of mine but we had had our wee run ins from time to time.

The problem with our Davy was that he had drawn up a hit list (due to paranoia) of his foes and was systematically sorting them out with violence. I had to confront him on occasions about his conduct, in fact it got to a bit of fisticuffs (at the bottom of Tambowie Street) between us over a family discrepancy where he had overstepped the line.

Having sorted things with him I tried to drive away in my Jaguar (yes I know, bragging is not allowed) when he jumped up and refused to let me move away.

"You're not leaving until I speak to you," he repeated time after time. I relented and let him come into my car.

What he said surprised me when he invited me to a Christian House Group that he had attended. I was silently pleased for him as he could not go on the way he was going and his enemy list was growing. So I listened and even promised him I would go (I did eventually go) to this house group.

So while I was lying in my hospital bed, Davy walked into my room with a shining face that looked like a Halloween cake, neatly dressed and with an air of freedom that was refreshing as it was palpable. All I could think was, "He has a court case or a wedding to go to."

But what I said was "What have you been up to, wee man?" He looked kind of shy, even embarrassed, which was not like him, as he approached my bed.

"I've brought you a book big man, it would be good if you read it," he replied.

I was so pleased at this obvious change, not only in his dress, but also his whole attitude – he looked good.

"Aye, what is it?" I replied.

"I have become a Christian and this book will help you," he said while still looking downward. All I could say, and I said it with genuine care was, "That's great Davy, I am so pleased for you." And I genuinely was.

At the same time I realised that I had cramp in both my feet as I had had my toes curled up in embarrassment for the whole time he was telling me about Jesus. He left shortly after and I was left lying in my bed with this book called *The Len Magee Story*.

Now then, the strange thing about this was that I had visitors daily but for the next two days no one came as far as I can remember. This time allowed me to read the book from cover to cover. Half way through the book I felt I had to put it down and listen. I did this and heard (not audibly) a voice say from deep within, "You are going to be a pastor."

I burst out laughing – I think it was joy expressing itself because it was a different laugh – as I thought to myself, "A pastor? I'm a Catholic and 'pasta' is something you get with bolognese."

A lovely warm feeling came from the laughing, which was being silently released from deep within. I went on to finish the book and put it down on my legs as I sat up in bed.

Then once again I heard the same voice, this time more challenging, more urgent and demanding a response. One word was said and that word shook me to the core. I knew who it was and I knew what it meant.

"WELL?"

I stammered and fumbled for words as I was being asked which way was I going and who would I serve.

It's only with hindsight as I discerned the word "WELL" that I can put an explanation on to paper, but at the time this is how I said "NO" to a question that meant, "Are you coming or are you staying?"

With all sincerity I silently said, "Lord, I have followed you all the days of my life. I have prayed to the saints and to your mother since I was a child. I am not that wealthy but I have enough to help you with the poor and downtrodden."

I was actually saying "No" in a ridiculous way to the Creator of the Universe. I was trying to do a deal with God, to let Him know that I could assist Him, wretched man that I am.

This episode faded into memory as I was released having recovered from my state of non-A non-B Hep. Things had become calm although I did feel weak, but the calm only lasted for a short season.

I did manage to keep my commitment to Davy and went to his house group just to encourage him, or so I thought. The seed planted was now being watered.

There are a thousand things each of us could write about our lives, and I know I am majoring a lot on crimes and mishaps, but there was a lot of love that came from my caring family.

I did find out many, many years later that my incarcerations had had an effect not only on my three wee sisters but on my parents too. Later I heard stories of family matters that I had missed, and of events I should have been there for, and was not. Alas, when you are incarcerated, your main goal is to get through and out.

The Duchess's car

After my stint in hospital I got back into the swing of things buying and selling cars from home which I enjoyed immensely.

I loved the way I would go and travel to see and buy cars for sale. I felt I was more than capable of that but I know pride comes before a fall.

One day I got a call from Thurso, in the very north of Scotland, asking if I would be interested on a Rover 3ltr Coup that had belonged to the Duchess of Rutland. Honest, that's what he said. I informed him that he was too far away.

The seller came back with a sales pitch that when I saw the car I would buy it at £600. He also said he was so confident of a sale that he would pay my train fare return if I decided not to buy. So I agreed and decided to fly up on a Loganair 20 seater plane after being assured that the car had not been in any accidents.

As the plane landed in a field (well that's what it looked like from the air) he was waiting to pick me up in the Rover. It was a great car but it had been resprayed and I detected a gap in one of the front wings, so I suspected it was a fully repaired car.

I knew that if I did not buy it I would be left with another plane fare back to Glasgow and only receive train costs so I was in a lose, lose situation. I spoke to the lad selling the car and said, "You are telling me this has not been accident damaged and I can take your word for it? But if I buy it at your price I will give it a full inspection when I get it back to Glasgow."

He was delighted with this offer, so I handed over the £600 cheque and left with the best driving Rover in the land. I then drove down to Inverness and spent the weekend with friends before heading back to Glasgow where I checked what I already suspected: the car had been damaged and repaired.

With this information I called up the seller and informed him of the damage that he must have known about, and invited him to Glasgow to pick up the car. I also returned the offer and said that I would pay for his train fare down to Glasgow.

He apologised and took £200 off the asking price. I was delighted and only wanted to put this in the book to let everyone know how much I enjoyed my work. I think I enjoyed the challenge of buying more than I did selling.

Back to hospital

At this time I was still using drugs, smoking dope regularly and hitting up now and again while still running my car business, but my tank was almost empty when I turned yellow again.

Straight to hospital I went without any hesitation and went through all the usual tests. Once again I was hospitalised but what I did not know was that I was supposed to take it easy and have complete rest.

From a young age I have always done press-ups in the morning and while in hospital I would do these when I went to the bathroom in the morning. This did not help my blood as it struggled to get through my kidneys and damaged liver. Once again I was released from hospital having been told that I had been infected with Hepatitis C.

Another side story to this revelation regarding Hep C was that there were a number of my mates who had used the same needles together, and they had also been diagnosed with Hepatitis C.

I remember getting a phone call many years later from a big pal of mine who had also been diagnosed, along with me, and a few others. The Hepatitis we were infected with had left its toll on my big pal and he was using a walking stick and his mobility was seriously impaired. I also remember clearly saying to him over the phone, "Listen, I know we all had Hep C but I gave my heart to the Lord and I am now clear, it's just something I know."

This declaration was said in blind faith as I believed I was clear. He said that to be on the safe side I should get it checked out. Being wise (not one of my strong points at the time) I made an appointment to see the specialist and had my blood taken for sampling. I was called back to the hospital on another two occasions just to run the same tests.

When I finally sat down with the specialist he informed me that it is not rare – but it is unusual – to find that somebody has antibodies that combats Hepatitis C. So my blood was clear, clean and free. As I walked from the hospital I knew that I had been blessed and favoured, yet again.

Perhaps I could write more about the months that were to come but I feel it's time to write why this book has been written, only to give glory to my Lord Jesus. So here we go on into my conversion and being born again.

10

A Phone Call Leads to Breaking Point

A day etched in my mind is when I got a call from Sammy. I was repairing a window on a car that I had sold him weeks prior. Apparently he had been in London on business and had missed his flight and he asked me to pick him up at Glasgow Airport with his car as he was arriving late.

I agreed but against an inner voice that was crying out, "No, don't go!" Running against this inner warning, when I picked Sammy up at the airport he then invited me to join him and go to Glasgow central station and pick up Jim, his courier, who was travelling to Glasgow by train.

Strange thing about this was that I had this gut feeling, in fact it was as if it was an internal scream, shouting out for the second time, "No, don't go!" But I heard myself say, "No problem mate."

When Sammy parked the car outside the station in Renfield Street I ran up the stairway and into the station to see if I could see Jim. On seeing him with his luggage, I pointed to the stairway leading down to the parked car.

What I didn't know was that Sammy had gone into another entrance of the station and was overseeing Jim and I. All three of us got to Sammy's vehicle at the same time but as we closed the doors we were surrounded by several plain clothed Drug Squad and Serious Crime Squad officers.

Only someone who has been used to being arrested knows that feeling of hopelessness and despair that crushes the soul. Even at this, however, my past encounters with the police would not allow me to give any officer the pleasure in seeing I was utterly despondent.

They had opened the bag with cannabis inside that Jim had brought up from London at the same time as two officers came at me from each of the rear doors – Sammy and Jim were in the front seats.

The two officers were high on adrenaline as they tried to search me as I sat in the back seat.

"Where's the tools?" (meaning firearms) one of them continued to say over and over in a high pitched voice. "What tools are you talking about?" said I laughing (yes, laughter is a defiance). "I'm not a full mechanic," I went on to say in a voice that hid the anguish I felt.

So there I was sitting in a police car being taken to Baird Street Police Office knowing that I would have at least three months untried to serve on petition. Finding out that Sammy had 33 pounds of cannabis in Jim's suitcase was certain to see me having bail blocked.

I knew, however, that the street law I had lived with and had practised all my life would now come into force.

The number one rule is that if caught you take the rap. So I knew that Sammy and Jim would stand up and be counted (even though there would be a three month untried period in C Hall Barlinnie for me) under this unwritten code of chancers.

So up to Bar-L we go. First couple of weeks everything was fine; lawyers sorted and interviews done regarding our statements. Then I got the explosive statement from Sammy when he said to me, "I am going to fight this charge!"

It may be hard to explain but his words crushed me as I tried to explain to Sammy that he was done bang to rights and if he went to trial it would only jeopardise my freedom. It was his car, his drugs and now it should be his responsibility to admit the crime. I was only along to do him a favour by picking him up from the airport in a car he owned and I was repairing. I was the one with the long list of convictions and that in itself would carry any prison sentences to a possible maximum.

It was as clear as mud, but even after weeks of trying to persuade him, he would not agree.

To my shame I threatened Sammy (Jim had already put his hands up and accepted that he was the courier) and that forced him to go into protective custody. This only made matters worse for me as I could not even speak to him now.

It was probably my worst time in prison, not that I was doing time, but a friend, a mate, had it in his power to release me when our court cases came up, and that friend had refused.

Usually in prison, as I have said, I am not one who can sleep the night away and being a Catholic I once again got into my "peace pacing" walking the cell hour upon hour reciting the rosary. This was in between planning what I was going to do and not going to do to Sammy. So I was sending prayers up and into the ether nightly while trying to plot against Sammy for his foolish decision.

Breaking points

Two breaking points awaited me during these three and a half months, and only by God's grace did I see both of them through.

I was on the pass in Bar-L, which meant I was allowed out of my cell to clean and cater for other prisoners who were locked up, this kept me busy and allowed me to go to the gym twice a week. It also allowed me to use an empty double cell on our landing as my private exercise gym and lodge. So with *'decades of the rosary'* and exercise this helped me keep a steady thought pattern that got me through those weeks and months.

"Clark, BAIL," came the shout from three floors below my cell as the reception officer called out my name and cell number. I couldn't believe it, bail for me? WOW.

Up I got thinking about what a wonderful lawyer I had and who knows, Sammy may have changed his mind to plead guilty, besides I really did not hate him anyway.

As I packed up my cell, all the guys, and even the prison officers, wished me all the best.

Down into reception I went, got changed into my civilian clothes and now just waited on the personal belongings and signature to be done. The utter relief and excitement you only get when being freed from prison (it's called "gate fever") was running through my mind in a flow of justifiable contentment, or so I thought.

"Ach, just forget about Sammy, what's done is done," came the passing relieved thought that I would have to have done something that I did not want to do.

And then phase one exploded in my face as I stood in front of the Reception Officer.

"I'm sorry…" were the words I heard but could not believe. "We've made a mistake, the bail is not for Patrick Clark, I'm afraid you need to go back to the hall."

The officer said it as if it was a "next, move along" situation, and on reflection I am glad I was stunned and did not know how to reply. As I was being led back to into C-Hall I didn't even remember getting changed back into my prison clothes.

As I went into C-Hall I told the Senior Officer that I was going to have a wee cell smash up at the injustice that had just been handed out to me. To his credit he told me the best thing for me was to be put into the observation cell next to reception.

Pacing this cell, with just a mattress on the floor, (no chance of a wee smash up in here), *decades of the rosary* and pacing did not help, but by the time the medic came in he was sympathetic and gave me the tiniest pill I have ever seen.

He said, "Here, take that – it will get you through the night and I will see you in the morning."

Breaking point one ...

This was the first breaking point.

This night of "the tiniest pill" was actually a nightmare for me. For whatever was in this pill, it was only by God's grace I saw it through with what went through my mind.

The injustice of the incarceration, the refusal of a friend's help, the thought of having to take revenge when revenge was not a part of me, could I hold on to my sanity when I told the officer that I was going to smash up my cell?

All these thoughts and questions piled up like a car crash scene that stagnated my mind in a condensed form. This all became a reality after about fifteen minutes of the drug taking effect.

Once the effect became manageable I realised that insanity is close to a human's breaking point. "How do I get out of this now?" I thought, realising that a sound mind was precious, even though troubles are geared to break mental stability down.

I never slept that night, dozing off now and then as I waited patiently for the medic to return the following morning. I was never so glad to see a prison officer as when I heard the medic ask, "Well, how are you this morning, Pat?"

Could he tell what I had gone through that night? Did he know what that pill does to people? So with an intake of breath I casually said, "Ach, I'm fine, it was just the shock of the false release that brought out those stupid threats about my cell." I was really meaning every word of it, but I was looking to him to see if he was persuaded enough to allow me out and back into mainstream prison without any follow up.

To my relief and slight surprise, he showed empathy towards what had happened the night before as he called out to his colleague three floors above, "One on third floor."

"On you go Pat, you'll be fine," was probably the best statement I had in those first couple of months, it was a massive release which saw me back into mainstream and normality.

During my time in C-Hall I had a number of visits from my lawyer John Morris, who is now a judge, and who had become a friend due to previous relationships I had with his legal company.

He hired my QC, a Mr Drummond, for my upcoming case at Glasgow High Court due at the end of our 113 day remand, which meant that we were at the end of legal untried incarceration deadline.

On my first visit to meet Mr Drummond, with John in attendance, the first thing he said to me was, "We will impeach Sammy." And before he had a time to say anything else I interrupted and said, "Hold on Mr Drummond, my name is Clark, and we don't impeach anyone."

(Impeachment is a process meaning I would have to say Sammy committed the crime as that was the only way my lawyers could then question Sammy in the witness box.)

"Oh, is that right Mr Clark?" responded Mr Drummond. "Well, let me tell you that if we don't impeach him, you are getting eight years due to your previous convictions, with Sammy getting five years and Jim getting four. So you make your mind up, for as your Counsel you need to let me know whether I go about this case my way or not."

I sat there, angry, shocked, and totally empty when I heard myself say with a bottom lip that quivered with self-pity and a touch of macho mince.

"Mr Drummond, I'll do the eight years but the last thing I will do is impeach big Sammy, I need to live with me."

Once these words were spoken I knew I had tied my flag to the mast and I could feel the ship gradually go below the water line.

My QC sat for a minute looking at me before turning and looking at my lawyer as if to say, "There's nothing I can do here."

Then he sat up erect, folded his arms and looked into my eyes and said, "Are these drugs yours, Mr Clark? Do you have anything to do with them?" It looked like a glimmer of hope but even so I had resigned myself to the eight years imprisonment.

"Mr Drummond, I had nothing to do with this bust nor the drugs, the drugs are not mine and never have been!"

Another silence followed as my QC went through a couple of his notes and sketches.

"Okay John," he said, turning to my lawyer, "this is what I need," as he pointed to one of his documents.

"A full exposed diagram and aerial photos of here and here."

To which my lawyer just nodded as he removed the sketches from Mr Drummond's pile of papers. Still dejected I then said, "Why do you want aerial photographs of Central Station?"

Looking up at me he put his pen down and said, "Look, this is a shot in the dark but it's a shot worth taking. Being in a car that

147

belongs to Sammy does not make you guilty. The drugs in the car are also not enough to convict you. What convicts you and brings in these two factors is what the police said they heard you say in Central Station. Do you understand that so far?"

"Aye, I get it Mr Drummond," I responded.

"Well," he went on, "two officers have given testimony that they heard you call out to Jim when you met, *'did you get the stuff?'* Now tell me, did you say *'did you get the stuff?'"* The meeting went silent again as Mr Drummond's eyes once again stared into mine.

"Mr Drummond, I said nothing of the sort. I only waved to Jim as he approached me," I replied.

"Okay, that's fine for me; so these officers are not saying what actually happened. Once we are in court I will have a large aerial photograph of Central Station and will be asking both officers to confirm where in the station you said the words *'did you get the stuff'*. Let's wait and see what they come up with."

And that was that, meeting over, a big sentence pending with a miniscule fragment of hope which did give me a bit of expectation especially when I knew that my QC actually believed what I had said.

With the upcoming sentence in mind I made some decisions. I had a nine-year-old daughter and a partner and it was them my thoughts went to.

At my next prison visit I proposed to my partner and she accepted – it took her a week to think about it, much to my surprise – even though she knew that eight years prison were pending. At the time I just wanted to do something right by both of them.

Breaking point two...

The big day came and breaking point two rose its head, but it's amazing what God can do. The nightmare I had with the tiny pill – my first 'breaking point' – came to my aid by way of experience, for it was that experience that kept me sane and ready to go one more lap.

They took Sammy out of his, by now, self-imposed protective cell to join Jim and myself in the prison van that took us to court. I was kept apart from Sammy in the van and also kept in a separate cell at the High Court.

No sooner was I settled into the holding cell when my lawyer, John, came down to inform me that there was bad news. Sammy had fired his QC as the QC said he could not put in a Not Guilty plea for him.

My lawyer was upset as we were at the stage where it became illegal to hold me due to the 113 days already spent in remand. The judge, however, had granted Sammy another two weeks to employ a new QC.

Upset? Aye, of course I was, as was Jim, for he just wanted to get his sentence started as we both were trundled back to our Barlinnie cells. Using the past experience of wrongful release I just buckled down and got on with my prison work.

Two weeks later we were back at the same court with the same separation precautions with Sammy. When we sat in the dock it was the first time in three months I could actually talk to Sammy face to face, but words were the farthest thing from my mind. Both John and Mr Drummond were deep in conversation before John got up and approached me. He beckoned me to lean over towards him and then whispered in my ear, "Don't sing any alleluias but Sammy has pleaded guilty, you are walking free."

Now, three and a half months of purgatory may have just come to an end but I felt more of a prisoner to hatred towards Sammy than I would have felt had I got sentenced to eight years. I had the urge to set about him as we sat in the dock, and as I contemplated this thought I heard the Clerk of Court say, "Mr Clark, please stand."

As I slowly stood upright the judge looked up from his paper-work and said to me, "Mr Clark, all charges have been dropped, you are free to go."

I walked out of the court into my family's arms after my QC had sat me down and told me the unusual story that led to my freedom.

Mr Drummond explained that Sammy's new QC would only take his case if he pleaded guilty as there was no evidence available for Sammy to be acquitted. Mr Drummond went on to say that, as he travelled through from Edinburgh that very morning, he had met the prosecutor who had informed him that one of the police witnesses who supposedly heard me say *"did you get the stuff"* had had a serious heart problem weeks prior and asked could Mr Drummond take this into account in his cross examination. My QC, however, informed the said gentleman that he was going to go in and be very hard as he knew that both officers had been economical with the truth.

The outcome of the court case was that Sammy was sentenced to four years imprisonment and Jim received three years.

All I can say following this episode in my life is that it was another step towards my salvation.

Revenge takes hold and Margaret makes a decision

On September 3, 1982, I got married to Margaret, but the scars of the court case hung heavily on and in my mind.

I don't know how Margaret put up with me, I was back at work selling cars but alas still using drugs. I think the saving grace for me in drug taking was that I could not get stoned during the day. I had to get my work done before I would dabble in different cocktails of dope.

It was obvious that our short marriage was fragile, which was totally down to me as I was besotted with thoughts of a revenge I did not really want to carry out. I wanted to close the book on

Sammy and the whole episode of what had happened, but self would not allow this because of all the threats I had made towards him.

I felt family bound to get even with the way he had shown me no care, respect or interest at all. Yes, I know, but in my confined mind-set, this was a matter of principle, short sighted and a foolish mind-set of betrayal. I know that now, but revenge blotted out all chances of reconciliation, even though that is what I wanted more than anything.

I'm off to India!

Christmas came and I had an old pal pay me a visit. He was a friend who was known to have imported some of the stuff I was ingesting. His visits to Goa in India had helped finance his small business. He went on to tell me all sorts of stories about Goa and how there was a large Christian community there and how they slept on the beach at night and preached on the streets during the day.

Now as we were both on another planet as we spoke, I got a picture of a Hare Krishna or similar type of sect that promoted free drugs and free sex, with plenty of rock and roll.

I honestly made my mind up before this friend of mine left the house, in fact I was glad to be alone to format my future plans that would incorporate Sammy. When he left I waited patiently on my wife and daughter's return from shopping. I sat Margaret down and hit her with a statement that was not only cruel but farfetched. All I can say in my favour is that I was consumed with self with no regard for anyone else.

"Margaret," I said boldly, "I've something to tell you." And without any rational thought or consideration, I blurted out, "I'm going to India." This statement had been birthed over a couple of hours by a stoned man's experience that gave me an answer to a problem that could so easily have been quenched by

151

forgiveness. Margaret just stared at me and said, "You are going where?"

"Look," I interjected, "I am going to India. We both know that this marriage is not working and I have things to do. So it's my intention to sell the flat, you and Tracy can apply for a house and then I will be off."

My plan was to stay in and among the sects of India for three years before returning for Sammy's release. I intended, under the supervision of my pal, to import substances on my return trip so as to cover my costs. That's how screwed up my mind was, but my God had other ideas and plans. I just remember Margaret walking away from me shaking her head.

So that was me sorted mentally as I had a new topic to take my mind off the obsession regarding Sammy. About three weeks later I was lying on the couch heavily stoned when Margaret came in.

"I just want to say something to you Pat," she said, standing upright to her full height of 5' 4" with a face that was glowing – just as my pal Davy's face glowed like the Halloween cake when he came to see me in hospital.

"Okay, you want to go to India, that's fine, go. I have had you to the back teeth and today I gave my heart to the Lord. I will find another place." And with that she left and went up to our neighbour's home upstairs for a cup of tea.

On my knees

I had never heard her speak so boldly and I became agitated but I could not move from the couch due to a heavy weight I felt on my chest that held me down flat. Not only that but I could not speak to defend my madcap plans.

It's only later in time that I understand what happened that night. One very large angel had held me down as he sat on my chest while putting his finger into my mouth and pushing my

152

tongue to the roof of my mouth. How do I know? Well, this was the fuse lit and it was going to change my life more than any big bang, for I was not being allowed to say anything to detract from Margaret's salvation.

Just lying there on the couch my mind swirled with the events of the previous months; drugs, courts, arrests, imprisonment, India, revenge, betrayal. The usual storm of thoughts were like waves crashing inside my head which were added to by the knowledge that Margaret had become a Christian.

Being so stoned all I could do was literally roll onto the floor and crawl into my small cold bedroom. Stripping off I quickly got under the cold covers and lay on my back. My mind settled as I returned to my old way of getting peace.

"How come Lord?" I asked in an audible whisper as my tongue had now been released. "How come," I repeated, "that I could see you in Davy and then I could see you in Margaret tonight? I have been praying to you all my life and yet you seem to be in them and not me."

A voice

After a short silence I heard His voice (not verbally, but the same voice I had heard in the hospital). By His grace and mercy He answered when I heard His voice deep in my soul. "If you are speaking to me, then get on your knees," came His silent voice that echoed through my whole being. The first thing that came to mind was, *"If I get up and get on my knees and Margaret came in what would I do?"*

Even at this special time "self" was throwing embarrassment and ridicule towards what I wanted to do. But I got up and kneeled at my bed like a wee boy and called to my Father.

"Lord, I've had enough," I said in a soft voice that suddenly seemed calm and in control. "I don't hate Sammy and I don't want revenge. I just want to be forgiven as I forgive Sammy and get on with my life. I want to change, Lord. I am sorry for my past life."

I was kneeling and I was repenting and it felt like the most natural thing to do. That's all I said but it was as if I had just breathed out all the storm of madness I had in me. I fell asleep straight away and slept like a baby. When I awoke the next morning I knew something had happened to me but even with this experience "self" was still adamant that I would separate from Margaret and go to India, or so I thought.

Small situations changed in the coming weeks and I saw things just that wee bit different – but the Lord was preparing me for a full revelation.

PART 2

Therefore if any man be in Christ, he is a new creature:
old things are passed away;
behold, all things are become new.

2 Corinthians 5:17

11

A Divine Encounter

March 1983

Goodness where to start? I suppose I need to begin at the point that all things became clear and real and that happened in my same, small, cold bedroom in the Glasgow district of Temple.

I need to start earlier in the evening. I had just purchased a Mercedes car and went to my young cousin's house to let him have a wee look – I think it's called showing off!

He had three mates with him in his house and they were smoking Temple Ball through a water pipe. Because I was driving I usually would not have bothered, however, I decided to join in. Within twenty minutes all four guys were so stoned that they were out of it. I just sat there for a while and even though I had taken my fair share of the opium pipe I was as straight as I had ever been.

I don't know why I felt angry but I just got up and left. I drove the car back home with no problem. Being that bit later coming home I just headed towards my bed. I noticed that Margaret was sitting at the fire with her bible (we had not spoken for quite a while). This, too, annoyed me as I thought to myself, "I'll bible you, lady… I'm still going to India."

This would be the last time that India would come into my mind until 2010 when I visited there with my youngest daughter, Brogan, on a church mission.

I had just put the bedside light on and as I turned I felt a hand from behind gently rest on my right shoulder. An intimate pressure slowly started to move up my body from toes to head. I noticed that the bright light behind me was so different from the bedside lamp at my left hand side that I had just put on. At the same time, and on reflection, I had noticed that this new light that was shining behind also went through me, as it produced no shadow of me at all.

Then, as this pressure started to move gently from my feet upwards into my legs and then my chest before resting on my mind, I don't know what I thought, but I did know that it was a deep spiritual happening. At this point probably a few seconds passed as the thought of a heart attack flashed straight in and then straight out of my mind.

It was at this point the pressure released itself through my eyes in a flow of tears that shook me to the core.

I silently wept for I don't know how long, probably only for seconds, but in that time I realised that the tears pouring from my eyes were from past sins, misdemeanours, all sorts of debris that I had been carrying throughout my life. At the same time I felt as if the pains of past hurts, rejections, incarcerations, regrets and sorrows were flowing out of my hot salty streams and on to my cheeks.

I was in no doubt whose hand rested on my shoulder, for now I was receiving the fruits of a heart change that had begun on the night I knelt before my God. I now stood on the same spot as I had knelt and said to the Lord Jesus that I was fed up with the way I was, and the revenge I was being forced to carry out due to pride. I told Him I did not want to hate anyone or hold grudges as I poured out my heart to the God I had been praying to for my whole life.

I told the Lord I was sorry for the way I had behaved in the past and was behaving in the present, all that was said only in prayer, now I was repeating it in my heart as a repentance. As I stood there with tears falling free I understood that there was something happening deep in my heart.

What I didn't realise was that the God of my youth (which had previously been just head knowledge, known to me as 'the Fanatic in the Attic') was being evicted as my Lord fell from my head to my heart, and that by repenting I was now being dealt with.

The dam breached – I was free!

It was the first time I had wept, really wept, but what I felt was the release, a release from my past as the tears carried this weight from my soul on every droplet that rolled down my face. Although a contradiction, it felt like a meandering tsunami of clear water washing me clean from the inside out.

This total release felt as if an abscess had being lanced before it could burst. The dam had been breached – I was free!

Then I heard a soft voice (not audibly) with the force of a flood say, "Tell your wife you are sorry."

This command was against my grain, for I had been right as I always was in all I did, or so I thought. I did manage to walk in and put my head around the living room door and say to my wife that it was time for bed. Now that was a breakthrough for me because always being right meant that I could not apologise first.

I remember lying on my back in bed and still wanting the tears to flow but I was too embarrassed to let Margaret know that I had been crying. I often have a laugh when I tell folk that I tried to cry out of one eye just so my wife could not see me.

When I arose next morning I knew I had to find out what had happened to me. I needed to know if what I had experienced was explainable. So as it was Sunday I waited for the masses to be said in Saint Ninian's Church before I went to the priest's vestry looking for answers.

There were a number of priests on duty that Sunday but when I arrived after mass was said no one, not one person, was at home in the vestry, including housekeepers. "So what next?" I thought.

Wee Davy was next in line because I now knew what the glow like the Halloween cake face meant. It meant the presence of the Holy Spirit.

His brother answered their door when I called and I found out that Davy, probably for the first time in his life, was on holiday. Where to next and who could I speak to? This was the question and the connection I desired.

I needed answers and I needed them straight away as I was apprehensive that I would lose this release as well as this revelation.

By early evening I found myself standing inside the Elim Church adjacent to my house. The building was open but there was no one there as I called out, even though the heating and lights were all on.

"Nothing left for it," I thought as I turned to Margaret when I got home and asked, "How many go to your wee "proddy" (Protestant) church?"

She took this question in her stride and replied that they had about twenty in the congregation. What she did not say was that from the night she had become a Christian this small group of Christians had been praying for me.

"Okay," I said, "I am coming with you tonight so don't be phoning them to let them know."

I feel kind of stupid writing this but it portrays my self-worth as if I was something special, but I had to put self aside as I desperately needed someone to tell me what had happened that night in my bedroom.

A new experience of church

As Margaret and I drove into New Life Christian Centre in Drumchapel I noticed that the car park was full. I remember thinking, "Twenty people? They must have two cars each." But unknown to Margaret another church called Glasgow Fellowship, with Rev Alex Gillies, had decided that day to surprise and bless the new fledgling church in Drumchapel by paying them a surprise visit.

I was about to enter a building one way and come out another, but that's not how it felt as we both stepped in through the front door. It was as if I had stepped into a vacuum as I was sucked into the centre of a gang of "loonies" with sayings of "Praise God, Hallelujah, and Amen" along with other holy words peppered in their dialogues and hugging actions.

I remember that when Margaret tried to walk away from me I grasped her arm with embarrassment and said, "If any of your 'proddy' pals say anything to me they are getting their jaws broke."

Goodness me, to say such a thing in a church just shows where my mind was – but my embarrassment was not to stop there, oh no, it was going to be stretched even further before it left. So as much as I wanted to renege and run like the clappers from this holy gathering I found myself sitting on the front seat of a full Pentecostal church filled with "nutters", waiting on the preacher to start his sermon.

I did notice that the expectant full house all seemed to have the same faces that resembled the Halloween cake expression.

There I was sitting exposed at the front of the "Amen Team," far too embarrassed to get up and walk out.

"Just sit it through," I thought when the pastor (who had come in with the visiting congregation) came on to speak, while trying to look as inconspicuous as I could.

Now as I said, the Pastor, Jim Kincaid, had come with the rest of the visiting crowd but what he preached that night was totally directed (it's called conviction) at me. I was really angry with every statement and story he told as I kept repeating to myself that my wife must have revealed these things to him. How else would he have known?

Final call

Getting near the end of the service I managed to calm down and just when Pastor Kincaid prayed a blessing over the congregation, the Holy Spirit spoke to me once again with one word.

"WELL?"

It was the same word He had spoken that day in hospital and now by His mercy He was giving me another chance.

In the depth of my heart I knew that this was a "final call" and as that thought permeated through my being, I had no embarrassment only an urgency to speak to this pastor.

"I need to talk to him," I said to Margaret, nodding to the small minister who had spoken right into my heart.

The next thing I know is that I was sitting on the front seat – while the melee of holy chaos was going on as the congregation were having tea – hearing conversations that ended in Hallelujahs and Amens.

I just had to talk to this man of God who was now approaching me with his hand held out. "It's Pat? What can I do for you?" he said as he held out his hand. Taking his hand we both sat down in a wee bubble of privacy.

I started to stammer and stutter.

"Look, I've been in and out of jail. I don't know how I keep going back. I do things I don't want to do, and I do things I shouldn't do."

Now that sounds clear but it was a statement of fumbles and stammers that made no sense at all, and to the pastor's credit he just said as he cut into my nonsensical sentences before pointing toward my face.

"Do you want to receive the Holy Ghost, Pat?" When he said that I knew that this was what I had been searching for all my life.

"I didn't know how then, but I now know why," I stammered. "Em, eh. Aye, I do." I said giving over the key that opened my heart.

This was the response I knew I should have made in hospital.

Mr Kincaid took one of my hands in his and my first thought was, "Oh no, he is touching me," and before I could do anything he then put his other hand on my shoulder.

Yet even at this point, when I knew something was about to happen, I was disputing with my will.

In a last call of defiance I could hear myself think, "He's touching me in two places."

But that was the last resistance as the dam broke through a dark heart as I heard the words, "Come Holy Spirit, fill Pat to overflowing, from head to toe."

While he continued to pray something started to move in my feet and I knew what it was. It was what happened in my bedroom. "Don't tell me I am going to cry and weep," I thought, but now it didn't really matter for I was being filled by a forgiveness that only God has authority to give.

(It's quite easy to write a book and put all the highlights with misdemeanours entwined, but my past held a lot of sin and

darkness and I also knew that most of that had ran down my face in my bedroom as He forgave me. The Apostle Paul wrote, "Wretched man I am, I don't do the things I should but do the things I shouldn't. Who will rescue me from this sinful nature? Only by the blood of Christ.")

Just like the first time in my bedroom, the presence of the Lord moved up through my body and into my mind.

The same peace, the same knowing was there but instead of tears came a deep cleansing that prompted me to speak in "tongues" instead of tears.

I was free, yes free indeed.

"Nikomo Seiko" I repeated time after time as the pastor stopped praying and started to laugh. "God bless you Pat, get involved with church and read your bible." And with that he went to speak with the rest of the folk whose conversations now sounded like angels singing.

I couldn't wait to get home, scared that I might forget the two words in tongues that I could not stop repeating. A major change had taken place in me and one of my main thoughts driving home was "wait till I tell everyone about this", so sure was I of a national revival. But in reality as I've often joked, half of my family thought I had had a nervous breakdown and the other half thought it was worse…they thought I had become a protestant.

Away with the drugs, smoking and swearing!

The first thing I did when we got home was to empty my wee drug stash by flushing it all down the drain and since that following week I have never gone back to them. I even stopped smoking, but the big thing for me was that I ceased to swear and curse. I always thought that I could swear politely because this was a habitual failing, since I would do it constantly no matter the company.

Not only had this salvation lifted me but I suddenly wanted to tell everyone about Jesus. This desire curtailed about 95 per cent of our house visitors which had seen friends calling every night, but now I was too caught up with going to church and a weekly house-group.

At one of our first house groups I remember being so filled with His presence I said, "I can't wait till the Lord tests me." The words of a foolish man…but even then Margaret and I got over and through those early weeks and months.

For the next few months I bedded into life as a Christian at the church in Drumchapel. One incident that brought me to the realisation that I had changed from my old ways of life was when not long after being saved, our church, called New Life Christian Centre, was involved with the *March for Jesus* event organised by Rev Alex Gillies. I was to be one of the ushers that walked on the outside of our marching congregation.

We left Drumchapel and marched down Dunkenny Road with "Jesus" placards as we sang songs to the Lord. I remember a couple of my friends looking out of their top flat window on Dunkenny Road, as we passed. When I saw them I knew they recognised me as they withdrew from the window, probably in embarrassment. Was I embarrassed? Yes, but only for a moment, as I knew that I had a battle to win with my mind (the fanatic in the attic) and no matter what, "self" will always try to dictate to my pride and status.

Ten years prior to that march, I had brought a carload of our guys (several of our gang, the Scurvy) onto the same road and chased away another gang (the Buck) from their base. On that journey to Drumchapel, I had travelled in the boot of the car so as to allow another one of our team to come along with us. One of the gang we chased was a cousin of my future wife as I was to find out many years later.

Both these events took place at the same location and on the same road. Change indeed. There was a revival at this time when around forty conversions took place including another two of my pals who dealt in drugs. It was an amazing time as we studied and meditated on the bible.

On one occasion I remember one of our guys making a statement in general and we then asked, "Where does it say that in the bible?" Yes, that was a time we had to get to church early to get a seat.

Myself and my pal, Briggs, walked over and into the police office that faced our church and spoke to the desk sergeant to offer our services in any way with the youth in Drumchapel (at that time we were doing football training on the church grounds). He stood back in surprise and unbelief to then nervously say, "Aye, okay, we will let you know."

We laughed as we left knowing the change in us was not recognised by our natural foe of the past.

There is so much to write about those early years that another book would have to be written but just to put in one other story that encapsulates the changes that had happened to this small gathering of twenty Christians that expanded almost overnight into a three figured congregation.

Another new member who joined us was Maurice Fieldman, he was into politics.

Maurice was and still is a bundle of fun to be around and during his testimony to me regarding his conversion from being an atheist, he informed me that he had a friend high up in the police who had made an enquiry to him regarding myself.

Apparently, this officer knew me and asked Maurice what I was up to. He asked him if I had bought the church and if my conversion was a sham as he thought I might have something that would need references pending a court case in England or abroad. We laughed our heads off but I think that was my first realisation that I was walking on a new path.

Mission trips to Paris and strange encounters

Around about August I had been encouraged by Rev Alex Gillies to go to Paris with Glasgow Fellowship on more than one occasion. I had declined as I was waiting to move house and had to be there if and when that would happen. Early on the Saturday morning I was out running and in conversation with the Lord at the nagging thought of Paris.

"Okay Lord," I said in prayer. "I will go if you sort out my house exchange." Arriving back home there was a letter from the housing department that confirmed my application for a home in the Summerston area of Glasgow had been successful.

That was that, Paris was on the horizon which meant by the end of that week I would be in France.

How on earth am I going to put into words the adventure of witnessing about the Saviour in a foreign land with over twenty folk from different churches?

Let me try…

Our bus left Glasgow and we managed to bond and blend by the time of our arrival. A memory statement was embedded into our being that stays with me today, *"Saviez-vous que Jesus est vivant et Jesus vous aime?" (Do you know that Jesus is alive and He loves you?)*

Our home was to be a church that was a converted cinema in the centre of Paris. The guys had the balcony area and the girls had the stalls as living quarters. I remember lying at night and saying out loud, "This is the biggest bedroom I have ever slept in."

I have been to Paris on two occasions organised by Pastor Alex and my next couple of stories come from those missions.

We had our bible study every morning and it was a great way to start our day. We then went out and on to the streets with guitars and tambourines. Our group would have a number of choruses followed by a few minutes of the Word before moving on to the next area up the road. This was a format we used while some of our team handed out tracts inviting folk to come to our evening meetings.

The very first day, I saw him. He was drunk but joining in with the choruses and dancing, to the onlookers' amusement. I knew he was heading for me as he slowly danced his way around to where I was worshipping. Once he was behind me he took a big kick that landed square on my backside much to the locals' amusement, before he danced all the way to the furthest point from me. He didn't look, nor acknowledge anyone before moving off as we went to our next position further up the road.

We all had a great laugh at my uncomfortable rejection with jokes that included comments like, "It's probably your singing," and such like.

The second incident went deeper and has shown me that evangelising is something that the devil has no time for.

On this occasion, I think it was my second visit to the same church in Paris, I led the group of twenty. We went through the same routine, singing, preaching, handing out tracts and then moving on. But on this occasion I took the team further up the road than we had been before. We came to an opening that was like a very large roundabout with a park and trees in the centre.

On the way to this area I noticed a young man standing in doorways but obviously following us. I put it down to him being attracted to what we were doing and the Word we were preaching.

We gathered into a circle at the park with one of the group playing a guitar as we sang a chorus. When we had done this, the young man came through our circle and walked right up to me. He was small with the darkest of eyes (similar to Mad Dog McGlinchey) and he raised his thin forefinger towards my face and said, "I have the power to kill you." It was proclaimed with a venom that even I could not recognise.

"Do you understand?" he went on, still shaking his finger slightly. "Do you understand that I have power to kill you?"

Now what was I to do or say as I noticed behind him that the group I was in charge of were getting fearful? I responded with, "We are just here to tell you that we love you and that Jesus loves you."

With these words just coming out of my mouth he pushed me with both of his hands that made me take a couple of steps backward. I remember thinking, "How come this wee guy has all that strength?"

What took place next was God's anointing as I saw it.

All at the same time, with despair and fear on their faces, I noticed our group was shaken.

Brian, my pal from church, was standing beside me, and at the exact same time we stepped forward in unison as we lifted pointed fingers towards this young man and spoke in tongues.

I then heard a barking that had to be from a pack of dogs fighting, but I could see no dogs as we kept up our verbal rebuke on our attacker.

To me he honestly seemed to shrivel under this rebuke and as he turned it was as if he slithered away like a serpent even though I did not notice our circle of believers break rank.

As he left the noise of the dogs subsided.

For a couple of seconds there was silence and then our guitarist started to play a chorus. It was one of the best choruses and highlights of that whole trip. Once the songs ended we seemed to all take a deep breath before somebody laughed and then the whole group joined in.

At this point a dove flew right into the centre of our evangelists. Yes, we knew that we had divine protection.

That night as we spoke and testified to those who were still in the church we were all as high as kites as we relayed the day's events. During that same night we were awakened by a shrill scream from one of the girls in the stalls bedroom below. When I awoke I saw a light behind the curtains that hid the redundant film screen.

This young woman from our team had seen a huge angel move above us and settle behind the curtains. On inspection the next day we found that there was no space nor lighting between curtains and screen, both were hard against the wall.

Any time I have been on mission I have always experienced Father's hand on what is being done in Jesus' name, so this incident just fortified the belief I have had as a child that God is with me protecting and watching over me.

Praying with a young boy

Coming home from my first trip to Paris we stopped in a massive car park once we got off the Channel ferry.

We all did our wee bits and bobs but as I was leaving the toilet area I noticed a small boy about seven-years-old with an older girl. I felt the Lord telling me to pray for this wee lad. My first response was, "Oh, no, not with all this crowd coming and going." But I responded with a challenge by saying, "Okay Lord, I will do it if I bump into him again before I go back to the bus."

So I contented myself with that outcome as I went on with my business until I bumped into the same wee boy five minutes later. I approached the young girl and said, "I hope you do not mind, I am a Christian and I feel that I should pray for this wee boy."

The girl smiled and said, "Thank you, he's my brother and he has a medical problem." (She told me but I can't remember what the problem was). All I knew was that as I prayed for this child and as the crowds milled and passed they noticed nothing.

I had been obedient as I prayed earnestly for this child's health. I left him just as someone else brought him a wheelchair and he disappeared into the crowd with his big sister.

I went back to the bus and sat quietly, a little drained but sorry that I had not made any farewell gesture to the wee lad himself. Just sitting there as our bus filled with my colleagues, we took our place in the long queue that waited in the busy car park to get back on to the motorway. Another bus pulled up alongside of us before moving forward. As I glanced across, the wee lad was smiling straight at me and waved. All I can say is it was a fulfilling experience.

So let's put Paris to bed and let you know that anytime I have been on mission I have come back blessed and free from burdens or stress.

A message for a stranger

I dropped Tracy off at school and headed back home to the new house we had been offered just before my first trip to Paris, as I was driving past a bus stop the Lord did it again as a lonely figure stood waiting for a bus.

"Go and tell that man that I know what he is going through and tell him not to worry."

"Oh no, not again," I thought as I moved into deflection mode. "Okay Lord, if this is from you and not me I am going to drive around the block and if he is still there I will tell him."

I must have taken ten minutes to finish my detour and was pleased to note that the man had gone from the bus stop. Everything was fine, and all I had been doing was talking to myself. But then I turned the corner at the traffic lights to see the same guy standing there – he had walked from one bus stop to the next.

So I pulled up, walked up to him and said as softly as I could, "Hey man, I'm a Christian and the Lord has told me to tell you that He knows what you are going through and that you are not to worry."

I left him there with his mouth slightly ajar as I heard him quietly say, "Who are you?"

"Just a Christian mate," I replied as I drove off. I noticed in my rear mirror that he just stood there with his head slightly bowed, whether in shock or in revelation, I really don't know. I do know that I felt I had to tell this man what was on my heart.

12

A Changed Life

Over the next couple of years my two brothers and I, along with a church friend, started a building business called *C-Saw Joiners & Builders.* I loved the work and the skills that were on display as I organised jobs and logistics. Unfortunately the small company had to close when we struggled to get enough work to cover our outgoings so we were left with a once derelict shop that we had purchased and restored, but still owing a mortgage on it. I took on the mortgage with the agreement of my brother and friend Joe to split the tools, van and trailer between them. This began another direction to my life.

Great Eastern Hotel: 1987

At this time my dear friend Eddie, who I had been on mission to Paris with, got me an interview with the Great Eastern Hotel on Duke Street. The hotel had begun its life as a proposed cotton spinning mill but ended up becoming a shelter for Glasgow's homeless due to the lack of demand for cottons.

As soon as I walked in the door I knew I wanted this job more than anything. The warm smell of damp and decay was like a hot breeze that took my thoughts back to Saint Joseph's Approved School when we had to walk in the corridors between the boiler room and the kitchen area. It had the same faint smell of cockroach powder being put down in a hot damp confined space.

Not being deterred by this, even as the overwhelming sensation of poverty had left the smells not only on my clothes but also on my mind, I waited to see if I had got the job.

Years later, when I left the hotel, I did save eight Day Books that had reports on all the comings and goings from the reception area. I will cherry pick a few stories as there was always a continuous stream of events that took place daily, from constant thefts to "skippers" (those who skipped in without paying), to fights and disputes. It was a busy establishment, probably due to the clientele that had a high percentage of alcohol problems and mental health issues.

"Start on Monday," said Davy, my new boss who seemed to be a city slicker by the way he dressed and not someone I expected to run a large hostel. He was fair and open to anything that would help make his job run smoother and benefit our residents. That suited me.

This imposing dark grey building was five storeys high, although the top floor was just a big empty space that was not in use. Four hundred derelict cubicles several feet high with some having overhead netting to stop any irate resident lobbing projectiles up in the air and landing on some unsuspecting sleeper, were available for rent. Only a third of these rooms had natural light and they measured approximately 8'x 6', around the same size as a prison cell.

Picture four rows of rooms running from gable to gable with two corridors. In the centre space, the two rows were joined, and the other two single rows faced the front and rear of the building. Only rooms in the front elevation of the building had natural light which meant that we had just the two narrow corridors between rooms. This was replicated on each of the four landings.

When I started we had well over three hundred men in the hotel, I think our highest number was over four hundred residents.

So there I was, part of a management team and I loved every minute of it. It took me a couple of weeks to settle in and devise what could be done to make living that wee bit better for the hotel clients.

On night shift, when I had time, I would walk around the floors (especially if we had any younger clients) and always seemed to catch or correct some of our residents who were not obeying the rules which were basic; no singing, no stealing and no drinking.

We had a common lift that carried the men to and from their rooms but most used the large stairwell. There was a main reception hall at ground level which meant that from our bowl-fish type office we could see all around and keep tabs on the lift, stairwell, recreation room that had two TV rooms, and entrance.

My first thoughts were to upgrade the living quarters, so I spoke to Davy, my manager, who in turn got back to me after speaking to the owner of the hotel. "Okay Pat," he said, "you can do what you like to upgrade the rooms but there is no money that can be spent, although we have applied for a grant to have all the cubicle windows replaced."

That was me up and running as I replied, "That's great Davy, and if I can get the rooms sorted will you agree to have them painted?" He just laughed and said, "If you can manage that, we will not only paint the rooms we will put flooring down too." Result.

Eddie and I also worked together with his idea of having a clothes boutique for the men whose clothes sense and cleanliness left a lot to be desired. So once again having permission from our manager, Davy, we got a lock fast room sorted out in the basement to hold donated men's wear. Now this basement area was just like the one at Saint Joseph's Approved School with a large steamy boiler room that was overrun by cockroaches.

Another small room in the basement was stacked to the ceiling with old clothes, suitcases and personal belongings that had been left by previous residents. The area also housed three badly stained cast iron Victorian baths in individual cubicles with each bath standing on ball and claw feet. The painted walls were peeling in sheets and the brick work was exposed, so the bathing area was handy for our donated "boutique" clothes store.

After discovering a few things that I knew I could help to change – not only the cleanliness but also the caring side – I took it upon myself to involve an NHS Senior Nurse (who went on to become a professor).

Changes and improvements

It was while walking the night shift corridors that I think I drew up my final plan when I saw that one of the cubicle doors was ajar. Quietly I opened the door and said to our resident who lay on his bed, "Are you awake, Mr Kelly?"

To which I heard a pitiful response of, "Hmm, aye."

Mr Kelly was a quiet man who would just come and go without a word. And as he lay there on the same type of bed I lay on as a sixteen year old in Barlinnie I asked him to sit up.

What I saw shocked me to the core. Mr Kelly pulled back the covers in obedience to my request and sat up. He had all his clothes on, including his coat that was buttoned up to his chin. As he stood up I noticed in the dim hallway light that on top of his thin mattress, which was covered by a rubber sheet, was a glint of dampness and a smell of urine.

"Oh Mr Kelly, you don't need to be like this," I said as I noticed the sunken bed springs. I was so filled with compassion at this quiet old man who always looked timid and shy, that he never complained and had to live like this unnoticed. We managed to get him sorted out by putting him into one of the newly reno-vated rooms and kept an eye on his welfare, but that incident still lives with me to this day.

William was different, he was the one that helped me decide to have a de-lousing programme.

He was a man who dressed poorly in "grimy" clothes but looked spotless. His face and hands always seemed to have a glow that comes with a good wash. But William was alive with lice that were so clear to see if you took time to look or notice.

Many of these men had mental health problems as well as phys-ical treatments that required a doctor. With this in mind I com-mandeered a room adjacent to our office and turned it into our wee medical centre that became our First Aid room.

So let me go through the favour my Lord has blessed me with as I tell you about each of these tasks that was carried out that first year.

Let's start with the big one. Where on earth was I going to get hundreds of beds and cupboards for the cubicles we wanted to put in?

I had heard/read something about Ravenscraig Hospital in Greenock upgrading or closing, I can't remember which. But with this news jumping out at me I called the hospital manager and explained my vision and our need for beds and bedroom furniture. The hospital were only too pleased to help us, and be-sides, it saved them storing and perhaps even dumping their old ward beds and bedside cabinets/wardrobes.

Within weeks we had the first and second floors painted, the new windows had been fitted as the grant had been passed, and the promised vinyl laid on the floor. The hospital beds and very narrow wardrobes fitted perfectly with a chair in each room.

It was so fulfilling to walk around the first floor which now smelt of paint, and the clean atmosphere had purged the dank smells of the past. This first floor was the jewel in the crown, so much so that we had hardly anyone move out. Mr Kelly ended up here.

Our second floor received the same furniture but we had to improvise with different beds. With the new flooring it meant a serious improvement for all the guys on that level too. All I could get for the third and fourth floor flats, however, was a coat of paint and a few beds to replace the bad ones.

The basement

Getting the basement sorted was easy as we had enough folk/cleaners to give us a hand to clean up the baths and scrape the walls of flaking paint. We never managed to get the brown water stains out but the baths were clean.

Two problems we did have down there was that the three windows, one for each of the three narrow bathrooms cubicles, could not be fully opened. The years of paint and neglect made them impossible to fully open beyond a couple of inches.

The other problem was although the hotel was badly run down, the heating system was always so hot that you could not touch the cast iron radiator pipes that ran through the hotel, especially in the basement.

Eddie and I had worked on his idea and secured our new *Eddie's Boutique* service with clothes starting to arrive, so that wee department was ready and set to go too with donations from local churches.

William and the Professor's 'wonder' potion

Okay, allow me to stick to this basement area for a while and explain how we evolved into a part time de-lousing, boutique supplier, and DHSS source of compensation.

Firstly, I was forced to contact our medical officer, John Atkinson, who is now a professor and a good friend, after I tried to help William in our first basement de-lousing bath.

As William got into the bath and sat down in the hot tub (with his underpants on) I noticed a plume of dark brown stain go through the water. "Oh, no," I thought, "he's just went and done the toilet in the bath."

I got him out straight away but he hadn't done anything of the sort. Allowing him to then finish his bath and using de-lousing shampoo I got him dried and changed before he went back up the stairs to his room.

I had noticed that William's skin was raw and inflamed in the lower stomach area and decided to call our NHS nurse John, who came over to the hotel and gave William a full examination. John took away an unusual sample of the lice that was living on William as he could not identify them as normal body lice.

We both knew that William had a mental disorder but there were no referrals nor outlets he would agree to us taking him to. After a time John came back to me with packages of powders, and what he told me made me more determined to get William fixed.

Apparently William had scratched that much in his lower region that the lice had taken residency all around his privates and backside areas. He had been infected with this problem for more than John cared to say. The lice were discoloured as they were living off the congealed blood caused by William scratching until the skin was broken and he bled. This also explained the discolouration of the first bath we had given him.

These packages that John gave me became an instant de-lousing solution not only for William but also for the dozen or so men we had in the hotel.

I had to put the solutions in the bath in a certain order and was a bit surprised to see the water froth up for a second or two.

William sat down in the water and I left him with the door ajar while I selected a new set of clothes for him. I can't say that I heard him singing, but as I put his new boutique outfit on his chair, he was glowing. I thought to myself smiling, "Goodness, he has been drinking this bath water."

He emerged spotless but his mental state did not allow him to appreciate what we all saw and how he looked. He, too, was put into one of our revamped hostel rooms.

Just to finish off with William, who always stayed in his room except to come down every few days to go and get supplies from the shops. On one occasion he came down into the reception area naked, got a coffee from our machine and headed back up to his room as if everything was okay. Unfortunately, when I was on night-shift one night (with one of our porters still on duty) William came down the stairwell and burst into the reception area at the side of the office. He was naked and shouting at the top of his voice. As I came out of the office to console him, he repeatedly started to scream, "I know who you are, I know what you do." He then grabbed the four inch main heater pipe that ran down into the cast iron Victorian radiator below. He was obviously being burned as the radiator and pipes were at their highest output of heat. I got him from behind and struggled to get him to loosen his grip.

I was quite a strong man in my day and I can honestly say that William was lucky to have had a third of my strength, but that was not how this situation felt. I was dealing with a powerful older man who matched my physical strength. I managed to prise him from the radiator and turned in time to see our night porter run out the front door in fear. He told me the next day that he was quitting as he was not paid enough for the job he was doing.

Finally, I got William into the First Aid room which was only twelve feet away, but I was exhausted after the ten minute of struggle and calling for the Lord Jesus' assistance as I came to the end of my tether.

Only when I did this did he stop his mantra of, "I know who you are, I know what you do…" as we were both entangled on the First Aid room floor. Then he exhaled from deep within and said in a voice that let me see his problem. "Help me, please… please help me," and with that I managed to get him up and onto the bench bed.

Pity and compassion rose within me as I knew that he had a spiritual problem that could only be dealt with by who I was praying to during those minutes. All I could say was, "Look William, you have a serious problem here. Can I go and call the doctor? It might be that you will be taken from here," I continued as he just looked at me and nodded, totally spent and defeated.

Covering him with a blanket I left the door open so I could see him as I called for our doctor who had an ambulance come to the hotel within a half hour of examining William.

William was wrapped up by the medical staff and taken away as the doctor got me to sign a form that I acknowledged that William was being committed for thirty days.

The next day I went in and explained to my manger and the rest of the staff what had happened with our elder resident William. They were all sympathetic but I felt really low except to say that his cry for "help" had consoled me and that I had acted in his best interest.

It was then that the porter came in and much to the staff's amusement he told them he thought there was a gang fight in the reception when he saw me and William struggle before he did a runner up the road, terrified. He never returned to his duties.

A couple of months later I was on reception when William walked in to book back into the hotel. While he was medicated he looked in good shape. I asked him if he was okay and he just nodded and then went quietly upstairs, as I got him a new room on the second floor.

The following day William approached me at the reception window and shyly said, "I want to thank you Pat. You helped me," before he walked away. It was one of those tear jerker times that made the job unique.

Over the next months I only saw William on occasion, and while he didn't say anything to me he just gave a smile and a nod each time he passed.

But once again, on a night shift he appeared at the reception window and said to me, "Pat, it is happening again."

I brought him into the office and asked if he wanted me to call his doctor. It was obvious to me that he was having another breakdown. When the doctor came with the ambulance to take him away he tried to smile, but I knew I would not see him again.

Big George

One resident, Big George, never looked as big as his name suggested as he was constantly crouched over, only able to get about using his walking stick.

Due to incontinency Big George stank like I have never experienced before. Due to his condition George spent most of his residency in our larger TV room. This was closed off to the recreation area by two doors and a large plate glass window which allowed management to oversee both TV rooms.

He would always sit by himself and took the daily abuse from residents, especially the younger men. Even in that, George would have plenty of space to himself as you could imagine on two fronts. First there was the aroma of neglect from his incontinency that was as pungent as it could be and the other was that George was an angry man when disturbed about his situation.

His heavy walking stick was not just to help him walk, it was more for swinging at any abuser who was stupid enough to get within striking range.

Now big George did not have lice so he could not join my weekly de-lousing classes, but he did need a bath because of his incontinency. So I decided to take him down privately after a couple of weeks discussing and persuading him about the new clothes we had for him and making sure not to mention his aroma.

We had been donated an expensive Italian style pin stripe suit that I knew would fit him, so I enticed him to come for a dip before I could part with the new clothes. The ploy worked and he agreed to come down to the cellar for a frothing bath – using NHS John's frothing concoction that made the skin glow. So on the day, down he came and into the cubicle to get ready for his submersion.

I took his walking stick and left him to undress in the steamy heat and the chemical bath that had settled into looking like real soapy water.

George had a long matted beard and sat crouched on the chair, but he could not get his trousers off and asked me for help (the bottom part of his trousers was stuck to his legs with dry excrement).

"O mammy, daddy," I thought. "How am I getting out of this one?" I mumbled to myself as I bent over to try and pull his trousers down before rushing out *boaking* at the smell, trying to hide my embarrassment by coughing and not to breathe in at the same time as not upsetting George.

"I cannot do it, Lord," I protested in prayer into myself. "I just can't do it," I repeated, trying to keep my face away from the cubicle where George sat. So clearly I heard, *"Whatever you do for the least of them, you do unto me."* That's what I heard and this is what I responded with. "Okay Lord, I will do it but all I ask is that you remove the smell."

I then inhaled and walked back into the embarrassed George. "Right Georgie boy, let's get this done," I proclaimed with boldness as my sense of smelling was totally filtered (even from the basement aroma).

So there I was up to my elbows in George's trousers not giving a jot. It was then that I noticed and felt the gentle breeze flow through the whole bathroom and it wasn't coming from the two inch gap in the window.

On reflection, and not by sight, I see a couple of large angels waving their wings to ensure that clean air comforted both George and I.

Having shaved and shampooed George in the bath, he emerged glowing, thanks to the magic bath solution.

We managed between us to get him dressed with his clean underwear and his expensive Italian suit. While bathing and shaving him, George told me he had been in the Scots Guards when he was young and it wasn't until he put on the new suit that I saw him for the first time straighten up to his full six foot plus height. He looked every inch a soldier of the realm.

Taking him upstairs no one noticed the new man that sat in the TV room on George's chair. But as the days passed his walking stick came back into use. Professor John and I had a discussion about him and it was arranged for George to go and see a doctor.

We found out that all that was required to sort out George's problem with his incontinent situation was a local procedure that was carried out within a couple of weeks.

Once this was completed we managed to get George into a care home in the city. I think he was as delighted as we were.

Malky

I need to put in a paragraph or two about another resident called Malky. Malky was a man who always had a dead pan joke to tell and spent most of his life standing at the reception's radiator.

He was just one of those guys who never let his circumstances get him down and always had a funny comment to every situation, although he rarely laughed.

His one bug bear was wee Wullie Jamieson who was just as funny as Malky but seemed to be drunk every waking hour. So there was always a wee clash of patter with Wullie going for the sarcastic line just to get Malky to move from his beloved radiator. One day a photographer asked if he could take photos of some of the Great Eastern residents and wee Wullie was chosen.

The photographer was doing a historical project of the old Glasgow and suddenly Wullie became a star of Hollywood proportions. It was a bit too much for Malky who left the radiator unguarded every time when Wullie appeared.

I got to know Malky quite well as he would often come home with me for Sunday dinner. He was a man who did not let his station get him down and had a mission just to make people laugh, and laugh we did.

Floods of water and claims

Our men were an amazing bunch and never short with answers and quips. Yes, there was a lot of heartache but laughter was intertwined. It certainly was a day of joy when a street water mains pipe on Duke Street burst and a tsunami of water headed for and gathered in the basement of the hotel.

Word got out that the storage area holding old possessions of former residents had been flooded. The next thing we knew damages claims came from half the hotel residents, swearing that they had left good clothes and other belongings in this room. All we could do was look at one another as DHSS and insurance inspectors came and took all their claims. All of the men who applied got their compensation payment and all got it on the same day, which meant it was a busy night for us at the Great Eastern Hotel.

Once the basement was dried out and boiler fixed we noticed that the flood had just about wiped out our cockroach population, much to my delight. The basement never regained its aroma of poverty.

'Soldiers' for breakfast

I was working night shift one night when word was sent to me from the chef (who lived in) that he was ill.

Goodness, how do you feed over three hundred men within a couple of hours? So, boldly I took on the challenge and with the help of one of the porters started to prepare. The good thing was that it was a staggered full breakfast that was served between 7am and 8.30am. I even managed to give the guys a wee bit extra by providing "toast soldiers" with their breakfasts.

As usual, the comments began with, "What's this? Soldiers? That's it lads – the rent is going up." All with much laughter as they ate. It was a full breakfast and good quality that was included in the rental of the rooms.

Every person had a story

There are many stories of heartache and of laughter but just to finish this chapter I will let you know about a Mr McEnena, an elderly gentleman. As the name suggests, he was a broadly spoken Irishman who kept himself to himself.

We would never see Mr McEnena during the day but in the evening he would make his way out from the hotel immaculately dressed to head for his pub.

At closing time he would return with a slightly redder face than when he left, which was the only give away that alcohol had been consumed.

He would then go into the games/TV room area and stand or sit next to the hot radiator and observe everyone without ever getting into conversation before he made his way back to his room. I always made it a point of saying hello, but without any major reaction except a nod from the quiet Irishman.

One night I managed to get a response from him and over a period of time he told me this amazing story.

Mr McEnena was an Irish navvy who had spent most of his adult life digging trenches and ditches in the Glasgow area. During the war he was taken to London to work with the bomb disposal team for the nation's capital city. His job was to dig around unexploded bombs so that the experts had room to defuse the mechanism.

After the war he came back to Glasgow and was awarded a medal for his work which he cherished. I did get a wee bit closer to him but he was a passionately quiet and humble man.

Then we had an older resident who was Polish, whose main aim in life was to go to the shops in the morning to buy broadsheet and financial newspapers while smoking his pipe. He was always serious but pleasant and easy to please with any requests he had, although I don't think I ever saw him smile as he walked about with his pipe in his mouth. I also never saw him with a change of clothing so he must have washed and worn the same ones for as long as I knew him.

One day we discovered he had died in his room; he was just lying on the bed in a room that was packed from floor to top of the partition with perfectly stacked newspapers. It was amazing how he had managed to get so many newspapers into this confined space. There was only enough room to squeeze through to the mattress.

Once the old gent was taken away our team emptied the room of the paper fire hazard. Thousands of pounds were found in his room, yet he preferred to live the way he lived.

Every one of our residents in the Great Eastern had a unique story – some we heard about and some we didn't.

Perhaps one day I will get around to putting the story of these amazing characters on paper too. It was a great time for me; a time of compassion, of reflection, of sorrow and for laughter too, especially laughter.

I also had the pleasure of working with a great staff including my two dear friends Eddie and Roddy. We also had Garry Lewis (actor) in our wee management team who was at drama school then. Yes, probably the best job I have been employed to do.

13

The Clark Gable Food Bar

While still working in the hotel, my wife Margaret decided she wanted to start work on a take-away business for herself. It was then that we looked at the shop we owned from C-Saw Joiners, it had been rented out but was now vacant.

We decided to turn it into a food take-away, it was next door to a dairy that her sister would end up managing. As our shop was already renovated and ready to go, I began to organise equipment and signage. I even managed to secure an old wooden fridge donated to us by the Great Eastern Hotel. I think I saved it from a bonfire.

About this same time our daughter, Tracy, was about thirteen and I had had a word from the Lord. It was very clear and I doubted it not. I felt my Lord say, "I am going to give you a son. He's going to be a special son."

And that was that. As a firm believer I believed, totally and without any doubt nor hesitation. I informed Margaret that she was about to become a mum again, and that we were going to have a special son.

She accepted this and we even decided on his name; he would be called Barclay. I made this prophetic claim to anyone and everyone who had an ear to hear. So I worked away in the hotel and managed to work in the shop all the spare hours I had.

We decided that it might be best if we could employ someone or that I should leave the Great Eastern Hotel and come into the shop to the new venture to work. Now this was a change and a challenge and the only way I could continue to work both jobs was obviously to get a pay rise, or leave the Great Eastern to concentrate on the business.

I decided to see if the hotel would give me a rise. I think I may have done that to see if I was a recognised cog in their business. But David gave me an emphatic "NO" as he was now being hampered to keep wages down. So for me it wasn't too hard a choice to hand in my notice.

It was exciting starting this new chapter in *The Clark Gable Food Bar,* besides, I had a new son that had been promised and would be on the way soon. (My name is Clark and the shop was in a gable end of two buildings, hence *The Clark Gable Food Bar.)*

On my last day at the Great Eastern I decided to take off my shoes and shake the dust from my feet. Not that I had any ill feelings, for there was none, but to just emphasise that I was finished.

Margaret and I both worked hard and started to make inroads to some profit when I had a visitor who offered to sell me his sandwich business. He had several customers and he delivered and sold approximately one hundred sandwiches per day. I asked if he would let me try it out for a week to see if it was viable for me to do along with the food-bar, which he agreed to.

I managed to do this and we agreed a price that suited me rather than him. Little did I know that this new venture (*Rolls Royale*) would grow massively over the coming years.

So there it was, I had left the Great Eastern, started working in *The Clark Gable Food Bar* while selling and delivering sand-wiches as *Rolls Royale*. Settled! Aye right, that will be the day.

Waiting for Barclay

By this time another year had passed and we were still working hard but our son Barclay had not made an appearance. So Mar-garet and I went to see a specialist in the Western Infirmary who assisted us with tests.

The results came back that Margaret had a gynaecological prob-lem and a hysterectomy was recommended.

I remember the day so clearly as Margaret and I faced the doctor as he informed us of this disappointing news. Yet inside my faith never faltered as I said to the doctor, "Doctor, we are Christians and the Lord has told me we are going to have a son." I know it shook him as I noticed his glance toward the nurse who was with him. "Who told you?" he asked just to make sure he had heard it right.

"The Lord told me," I declared before adding. "My God doesn't need a womb to give life, but Margaret and I have decided to leave the womb in place because we believe that we will have a son."

He looked as if he was going to explain something that was fall-ing on deaf ears but he went on.

"Well Mr and Mrs Clark, I commend your faith, but I am here to give you the facts. I wish you both well in the future." And with that both he and the nurse left.

A few months passed as we both worked in the food bar when we got a second letter from a gynaecologist called Dr Drum-mond (yes, the same name as my QC at Sammy's trial). It was a letter proposing an appointment to meet with Dr Drummond. This we duly did and when we met she informed us that they had a new procedure and technique that involved micro surgery which allowed them to go in through the tummy to have a look to see what problem may be there. It was a fragile procedure that she offered to carry out. Margaret and I agreed, so Margaret was admitted into the Western Infirmary within weeks.

After the procedure Margaret had to lie still for a day or two before release due to the fragility of the new technique. A further couple of months passed and we received a new appointment to go and see Dr Drummond regarding her surgical investigation.

On arrival she had us sit comfortably and then gently explained the findings of the procedure she had performed.

"If you can imagine the fallopian tube is tiny and at the top of this are the smallest tentacle like fingers. When I touched the first fallopian tube it began to break away. Touching the second one, I knew it was going to go the same way, so I just left that one alone because my diagnosis is to confirm the first doctor's diagnosis. You do really need to consider a hysterectomy, Margaret," she finished saying as she looked at Margaret.

Margaret just repeated what we had said to the first gynaecologist and as we stood up to leave, Dr Drummond said, "Pat and Margaret I am a Christian too and I commend your faith." And with that we left.

What we didn't know was that when we met with Dr Drummond that day, Margaret was one month pregnant with Barclay.

Our special son was already on his way, even as we spoke to Dr Drummond, and about time too.

I don't know how Dr Drummond got to know about the pregnancy but she got back to us many months later and informed us that although she was not a drinker, she had allowed herself a wee bottle of champagne when she heard the good news of Barclay's expected arrival.

Another business

With Barclay finally on his way and our sandwich business beginning to grow along with the snack bar, the snack bar had reached an income that attracted a buyer who made us an offer we could not refuse.

During that coming year it was all hands on deck, and I decided that we should take on a restaurant in Drumchapel.

So by the time Barclay was due, we had secured the lease for the large restaurant in Drumchapel and I was upgrading this, the new cafeteria, along with running our two existing businesses – the snack bar and sandwich run.

The cafeteria was renovated and almost complete as we had pencilled it to be operational and open around September as the moving in date by the new owners of our shop drew near. We had sold the wee shop with the intention of using the new restaurant premises in Drumchapel not only as a restaurant but also to expand our sandwich outlet in the upstairs main hall, the room that the sandwich company needed to grow.

Barclay arrives – September 27, 1989

I remember the day that Barclay was born so clearly. I had been in the shop that morning at 2.30am to make and deliver our sandwiches. When I returned from delivering the sandwiches I was preparing the foodstuffs for the food bar to open and Margaret walked in. She was in labour, but after my initial panic settled she persuaded me to let her work the whole day.

Yes, she got through it with flying colours but we left the shop after six o'clock to head for the Yorkhill Maternity Hospital in expectation of Barclay's arrival.

Driving up to the hospital I suggested to Margaret that I would go in and get some odds and bobs from the shop to see us through the night of labour. Margaret got the lift up to the ward and I was just behind her.

By the time I got there Margaret had been taken directly to the labour suite. When I arrived, five minutes later, we knew Barclay was on his way. It was just before seven o'clock that we got settled into the labour room, then Barclay arrived at 7.20pm much to everyone's surprise.

I describe his delivery as his entrance into the world, but it was as if Barclay literally shot into the world, however, I doubt if Margaret would agree. I'm almost sure that if the midwife had not been there to catch him he would have banged his head on the bottom of the bed.

What a feeling it was to hear it proclaimed and confirmed that Barclay was a boy and that was accompanied by our son's soft cry. Within minutes this wee promised bundle was in my arms cleaned and wrapped up in a small sheet, ready for our inspection.

As we were left alone by the midwife and staff (which I found strange, but it allowed us to give thanks to the Lord), I just held Barclay above my head and prayed and proclaimed, "Father, we thank you for this gift that you promised us, and as I give him back to you in this dedication, we will look after him in Jesus' name."

It was short and very moving and we did not notice the length of time we had waited for Margaret to be attended to. I had phoned our pastor who was holding his house group meeting and who were so delighted going by the noises I could hear from them over the phone.

I left the hospital after ten to go home and be with our daughter Tracy (who was now sixteen), whom I couldn't calm down from the excitement of having a wee brother. It was then I got a call from the hospital to ask me to return so that we could meet with the paediatrician.

I immediately called my pastor before I left our home to get the house group to pray for us as I jumped into our van and drove as quickly as I could back to the hospital. When I got there Margaret had been put in a single room and was holding Barclay. She told me that the doctor wanted to speak to both of us at the same time.

A 'special' son

When the doctor came in she said, "I'm sorry to say that we believe your son may have Downs Syndrome."

I looked at Margaret and then my son and did notice that his beautiful face was a face of angelic contentment with Downs included. I didn't know it was possible but I seemed to love him even more now that this news had been given to us.

"What do you feel about that?" the doctor seemed to direct the question to me. "I don't know how I feel doctor. Is he Downs or is he not Downs?" was all I could say.

"We won't know for definite until we get the results back, but we think he is." She told us to let her know if there was anything she could help with and that she would be available. She then left the three of us alone.

So that was why the delivery nurses and attendants had left the delivery room so early; they needed to get a paediatrician before they could give us this information.

I don't know how long I sat for but to my shame I fell out with Margaret that night as I totally focused on Barclay and where were we to go from where we were.

As I walked down the dark corridor of the hospital heading to go home, I saw a silhouette figure in the distance who was my pastor.

He asked about Barclay and had come to support us, but I was numb and just wanted to be by myself, although his gesture was really appreciated.

As I drove home I had a confrontation with my Lord and my God. I don't know if it was anger or emotion or perhaps a bit of both but I had questions I needed to ask Him.

As I drove along the words came from deep in my soul. "How come Lord?" I shouted aloud as burning tears welled up before overflowing onto my face. These were tears of a son seeking an answer from his Father. "I told everyone about your promise. Why Lord? Why? You told me he was special, You told me he was special," I shouted. This question was repeated over and over as I sped along the Clyde Express Way.

Wiping the tears from my face my Lord and my God spoke to me in a way that only He can. The reply came as a soothing balm that halted my tears when the Holy Spirit spoke into my heart.

"He *is* special Pat, just wait and see."

When I got home Tracy saw that I was drawn and asked what was wrong. "Your wee brother has Downs," I informed her.

She just looked at me and for the seconds it took for her to take in this news. She looked me straight in the eye and boldly and passionately said, "I don't care what he has got dad. He's my wee brother and I love him." She then ran upstairs to her bedroom. That's the kind of effect Barclay has to this day.

Tracy and Barclay

Even though Tracy had not even seen her new-born brother, she loved him with a compassion that can see past any problem.

How was I to know that this baby would become the joy of all my family's lives? How was I to know that what seemed to be a major crisis would be the best gift I have ever received? Who can say that their thirty-year-old son jumps into bed in the morning, plants a big "slobbery" kiss on your cheek and says, "I love you, dad?" He is a blessing that has not been surpassed and I give the Lord all the praise and glory for such a gift, for such a son that is so special.

Barclay had a few problems with his health. Heart, hips and stomach would all need to be addressed with major surgery in the coming years but as for now he was taken into intensive care to get him through the first few days and weeks of his life.

I would go up every day, take his hand in the incubator, and tell him I loved him. For the next three days I was in a bit of a stupor and just spent my time working to get the final touches of the restaurant sorted for opening day (the food bar had now been sold).

I wasn't sleeping and by the time Saturday came along I was washed out with thoughts of how Barclay and I were going to fit in along with a lot of other nonsensical thoughts.

Two of my pals from the hotel, Roddy and Eddie, came up to my house that Saturday and bullied me into going to see Celtic play at Parkhead, just to get my mind off things. I reluctantly agreed and we were among the first people in the main stand to arrive with over an hour to kick off.

The two lads stopped to get a coke at the kiosk and I just walked slowly up the stairs with them trailing me. A young boy was just in front of me and when he got to the top of the stairway he turned and smiled at me. He then just walked on and into the sparse stadium. Now that was nothing in itself; he had on a Celtic scarf but when he turned around I saw that he also had Downs. That was the moment I had breakthrough – three days after my son was born.

As my two pals joined me I asked them had they seen the young boy in front of me but apparently they hadn't. So I ushered them up into the stand and said, "I will show you." But there was no one there except a few adults.

Whether that wee boy was there or not I don't know but it was something I saw and accepted, and from then on I knew that everything was going to be just fine. I could take my son to football and anything else he wanted to do. I said to myself, "Goodness, let's get him out of hospital. Let's get him fed and clothed and loved."

And that was that.

Another promise

Five weeks later Barclay came to church for the first time. That day stands out as Margaret held him in his shawl and we sat in the same seats that we sat on the night I became a Christian.

There was a chorus being sung and as I looked at Barclay I noticed a tear drop from Margaret's cheek and on to the shawl that held our baby. Just at that point, my niece Teresa (now one of the congregation) came behind us and whispered, "The Lord has shown me that there is another baby on the way."

We said nothing but we did believe.

A few years later we had a wee cracker of a daughter and we called her Brogan. What I can say, is that, what I have witnessed through the love that Barclay attracts, is special.

Brogan

I adore my two daughters and grandkids but there is something that Barclay has given to me (and my family) that takes this love up a notch. It's called compassion, and compassion is what takes love up to a higher level.

Now I know how much God loves me. I now know what compassion feels like. It's a love God has for His children and it's called *Agape*.

Barclay had his three major operations in his childhood and he is doing fine.

Clark Gable Food Bar and Rolls Royale 1990

We now had a restaurant of seventy covers and an upstairs that was big enough to put in conveyor belts to deal with the expansion of the sandwich company. Within the year it was obvious that the café was being subsidised by *Rolls Royale*, so something had to give.

It was always my desire to have a full complement of believing staff which would allow us to have a group time of prayer before we started work. This lasted for about a week when I went upstairs to find two of our believing staff battering lumps out of each other. That bump on the head experience just meant that my prayer time would be done alone.

One day I received a VAT bill and it was obvious that I could not meet its demands so I approached one of our congregation who was an accountant and offered him half of a company that was just keeping its head above water, to join me. He agreed and told me that the restaurant had to go.

With no buyers available we were approached by *Drumchapel Opportunities* who were delighted to take on the restaurant for the cost of our VAT bill. They planned to turn the restaurant into a training centre for the unemployed and run it as a Public Enterprise.

We were delighted as they had made clear to us that *Rolls Royale* would need to commit to continue its operation from the above space that we were using. That was easy to agree to.

Although *Drumchapel Opportunities* were getting a good quality fitted out restaurant with kitchen, we would benefit with the guarantee of a rent free tenancy in the upstairs hall.

Deal done, problem over. Aye right!

Unfortunately for us, the management of *Drumchapel Opportunities* (OG) had overspent and we were the ones that their committed promise of having our VAT bill paid was now reneged upon.

We ended up just passing the restaurant over to them for free but the VAT put us to the sword and we had to reconstruct the *Clark Gable Food Bar* structure when we closed the company down. We then invited Stuart (my pastor) to join us and he became the third partner in *Rolls Royale*.

We worked hard and made headway with the help of the free rent but I felt we needed our own place.

I sourced an old derelict factory in Maryhill and started to make enquiries when we were approached by Charlie Gordon who was the local councillor. Mr Gordon had got wind of our intentions and was keen to keep the jobs we provided in his Drumchapel catchment area.

He went on to say that he (the local Council) had a factory in the area that they had a lease on, and if we were interested he would get us a grant to refurbish it. This was a no brainer and after seeing the 5,000sq feet building, I was sure I could renovate it into a working unit that would suit our hygiene needs. What he didn't say was that the rental for the factory was something he as a councillor wanted to financially pass to someone else, so he had two birds with one stone.

The rental was a wee bit high but we felt we could afford it.

I started the renovation and within a few weeks we were almost ready to get our equipment brought in and fitted. All we needed now was the promised grant to start our operation.

I was advised to miss the council meeting by my two new partners as they, like me, thought the grant was a formality.

Mr Gordon had stood up and recommended a grant for *Rolls Royale* due to the fact that we were employers of the district and this goodwill gesture would cement our commitment to the area.

The Chairlady asked if this grant was just a sweetener and I don't know what Mr Gordon said, but at the end of the meeting all we got was a £10k grant that had now become a loan and had to be paid back.

At the time I was angry and felt as if we had been conned but we buckled down and got our state of the art (for its day, and that's my interpretation) factory up and running.

I worked hard at that time doing up to eighteen hours per day on occasion and this led to the breakdown of my marriage.

I would basically get home, fall in the door, see the kids and get to bed for a few hours and then start again.

I remember one night I was so tired but because we made our sandwiches on night shift (to keep them as fresh as we could) I just collapsed on the bed fully clothed.

Within an hour I knew I had to get up and go back to the factory.

I forced myself to rise up, get washed and get back into work. I overrode my body's desire to sleep. That was a night I knew I had done myself some physical harm by refusing to rest.

During this time our prophesied daughter, Brogan, arrived to our utter delight as our older daughter Tracy had given birth to my grandson Dylan whose dad was one of my managers at *Rolls Royale.*

Our family was complete and in this I had contentment. I religiously took my two kids out every Saturday afternoon as this was the only time I had free.

I took them to every swing park in Glasgow and as far as the caravan parks from Port Seaton to Aberfoyle.

There was a wee bonus in this for me, not only was I having the company of my kids I could also listen to the football from 1pm to 5pm.

Breakup

Over these years Margaret had had enough of me. And rightly so. One day, after we had had a row, she stood to her full height of five foot four and told me she was done with me. I thought it was just one of the usual arguments we had on a regular basis. But she was serious.

A year later, Margaret got a house of her own and informed me that she was going to go and take the kids. There was no way I was going to allow that. We had a good home, I had a good income and the kids wanted for nothing.

"It's not happening Margaret," I declared. "You can go but I'm not giving up the kids."

"You have not helped me once to get my new home sorted," she informed me with tears.

All I remember after that was having a quiet time with the Lord and hearing Him say, "If you want to keep your children, then let them go."

I then heard myself say to Margaret, "Okay, I will help you to go. Are you ready?" She nodded as I went on. "I'm going to get a van, get your stuff together. I will help you right now. You can go."

"What about the kids?" she asked. "They can go too," I heard myself say with a sinking feeling.

I moved all of Margaret's belongings with two van loads that very afternoon and then returned the hired van. Both Barclay and Brogan joined their mum in her new house. I then went to B&Q and bought paint and brushes.

It was Christmas Eve and for the next three days I painted my house from top to bottom as I could not dwell on my loss.

Now, years later, I have a better relationship with Margaret than I ever had. She is a good friend and still a great mum. Our break up was entirely my failing due to my neglect of her, and I am pleased to say that she has forgiven me.

A brush with death

At the height of production in the factory we made just under thirteen thousand units including sandwiches, rolls, batons, salad boxes etc per day. We had five vans that delivered right through the central belt of Scotland.

One lifesaving experience I had was when we were a driver short. I did the Falkirk/Edinburgh run and had Andrew, one of my employees, join me for the run as he had nowhere to go after he had finished his shift.

It was a frosty night but the driving conditions were fair. Early in the morning, as we drove past Falkirk on a country road, we went into a dip in the road which had an embankment and ditch on either side. It was also heavily wooded with large trees on both sides. It was as if we had driven into a dark tunnel when suddenly the van went into a side skid as I turned into the bend.

We seemed to pick up speed as we headed for the thickest tree in the wood. At the same time as we crashed up and onto the embankment, with only the tree able to stop our out of control voyage, I looked at Andrew to see a fear in his face that had to be addressed.

"Jesus!" I called out as loud as I could and we halted immediately as I heard Andrew exhale loudly. It was a miracle neither of us was injured and I know you will already have guessed that I gave thanks to the Lord.

I called my two partners who met me at the next delivery point. I managed to reverse the van down from the embankment and get into the next drop off point. The van was badly damaged but drivable once I had hammered all the front panels away from the wheels.

Selling and moving up in the world

Not long after this we were approached by *Hamilton's Dairies* who enquired if we were interested in selling *Rolls Royale*.

Hamilton's had sold their business to *Wiseman Dairies* and were now looking for a sandwich company to purchase. By this time all three of us decided to see what they were offering. I for one wanted to move on. I was just tired.

We had a meeting planned with them in a Glasgow Airport hotel and by the time I got there, they were ready to negotiate. That day I had just secured NHS contracts for the Central belt of Scotland to supply them our sandwiches and rolls; we sat in front of their team and they offered us £120k for our company. We then informed them that we had just won the contract from the NHS. They then had a discussion and upped the offer to £150k. That was acceptable for me for it covered my original investment when I had sold *The Clark Gable Food Bar*.

"Afraid not, Pat," said the new purchaser of *Rolls Royale*. "If you decide to sell to us, then you need to come along as we plan to build a brand new £2m factory in the expansion of *Rolls Royale*."

As much as I wanted to leave (that very day would have suited me) I knew the deal included the three of us partners. We agreed and were paid one third each.

Our wages were upgraded, along with a company car and all we had to do was keep the wheels turning.

With the contacts our new chairman had, we supplied sandwiches for *The Open*, the Queen's visits to Scotland along with a few high market race course gatherings.

The new proposed factory drawings had been completed and I was asked if it should be built in Drumchapel or Kilmarnock. I informed the new board that we had been let down with the local councillor's broken promise. When they came to their decision the dye was cast.

They had agreed to have the new factory built in Rowallan Business Park by Kilmarnock. So for the next year we just kept working away as the new factory was being erected.

They had given *Rolls Royale* a new name by calling it *The Sandwich Company*. I accepted their decision and travelled to and from Kilmarnock every day.

I disliked the job immensely even though I had my own private office, entry key, company car and a receptionist who once called me Mr Clark. It was just not my cup of tea.

The Sandwich Company has changed hands more than once since, and I noted that they finally closed the Kilmarnock plant in December 2018 and moved their operation to England. (See below).

It had taken a long road from *The Clark Gable Food Bar* to where it ended up.

Local news report

The Sandwich Company factory in Kilmarnock

The Kilmarnock jobs market suffered a hammer blow this week with the announcement 180 jobs are expected to go at Adelie Foods.

Staff were told the news on Thursday morning by operations director Alan Stirling – an inside source said it will affect the company's two sites in the town.

That will see the company "move volume" from its Kilmarnock factory to its "southern sites in Wembley and Southall" from the start of the New Year.

Confirming the news, which comes just 11 days before Christmas, the company's chief executive said the move will future-proof the business.

14

The King's Court

As soon as my payment for *Rolls Royale* came through, I had decided I wanted to go for a property to renovate. As I only had to work at Kilmarnock five days per week, and most of this was on the road, I had time to do my homework.

I knew that the Faslane Naval base had cut back on their Naval commitments and a lot of USA sailors had returned home which left a glut of homes for sale in the Argyll area. So this was the target area I concentrated on for property. And sure enough there were plenty of homes for sale.

With the money from the sale of *Rolls Royale* and with the disappointment of not being able to secure two properties in Dunoon that I had bid for, I then went to look at the advertised building that I saw in one of the estate agent's office brochure.

The Adolphin building

Driving down to Tighnabruaich was a pleasant Saturday morning drive even though the weather was a tad drizzly. I had sourced an old derelict tenement called *Adolphin Building* in

Tighnabruaich which housed four families. The building itself was in a desperate state of repair.

I loved the premises before I even stepped inside to view it. On the brochure it resembled an old Glasgow tenement, and that is what it was, with three floors.

I met with the owner, who owned another house in the area. He was delighted that I was interested in restoring the building due to the problems he was having regarding forced repairs and an uncooperative tenant. We agreed on a price and I paid half up front with the agreement that the rest would be paid on completion of the property. He understood that my budget would barely get the job done. So the old *Adolphin Building* was about to undergo a serious renovation.

I planned this renovation to be complete within the year. Alas my enthusiasm did not match the zeal I had excitedly predicted.

After borrowing from a relative to keep the renovation work going, I found myself under pressure to pay the remaining money that was outstanding for the house, even though it was not complete.

I had to use my car sale skills when I got the chance to buy a really expensive car at a cheap price, just to keep the ex-owner of *Adolphin Building* content for a while.

I was still working at *The Sandwich Company* when I ran out of funds, so reluctantly I stopped all the final work at *Adolphin Building*. I still owed my relative money and also had a two thousand pound payment outstanding for the purchase of the property.

On one of my last visits to Adolphin before closing the work down, I was running upstairs to the top floor when a pain thumped into my chest and arm as if I had been punched. It felt as if my upper body was in a vice as I was slammed against the wall. I knew that this was a bit serious and made an appointment with the doctor as soon as I got home.

I was sent to hospital straight away and after tests I was told that I had a narrowing of the arteries. More tests came and went as I was put on a cocktail of drugs and told that I would need to stop working for the time being.

Apparently I had three blocked arteries; one artery 30 percent, one 60 percent and one 80 percent blocked. It's not that the arteries were blocked in a real sense, it was more because my arteries were more narrow than normal.

My Ma's family of six siblings had this problem with the heart. Three of them went on to have heart bypasses.

So there I was with a cabinet of pills and a meeting with the Director of *The Sandwich Company* to tell him I had to go on sick leave.

The Maxie Richards Foundation

I recommended a lady who knew the job to take my place until I could get back. Taking the medication was a nightmare for me as side effects hampered my whole sleeping pattern. My weight went up instead of down and I had to go back to my doctor and inform him I could not live like that.

More angiograms took place and my surgeon told me that I needed a by-pass. They were trying to treat me with medication but it was obvious that my preference was to go ahead with surgery and my surgeon agreed that it was probably the best option. Done deal.

During this time I had a really close tie in with my Mum as my Dad was showing signs of Alzheimer's. It gave me a chance to show her more of the love and appreciation I had for her.

While waiting on the operation I had started some voluntary work with *Maxie Richards Foundation,* at the same time I heard that *The Sandwich Company* were about to buy out one of our sandwich competitors. With this in mind I phoned the Chairman and offered to come in part time until I got the all clear, however, he wanted me to go back on the road to get more sales. I told him it didn't suit me to return to travelling and that if he made me up a package I would be willing to leave – I would have been delighted.

They then made me an offer which I discussed with Margaret who encouraged me to accept, so I phoned them back and accepted instead of waiting days to decide.

The Chairman asked if I could meet him at the Rangers car park in Govan. I was allowed to keep the company car and was given a £12k cheque severance payment, much to my delight. This money was spent on the house at Tighnabruaich and that was the last straw for my much maligned wife.

So there I was, new heart getting arranged, enough money to finish Adolphin at Tighnabruaich and working voluntary at the *Maxie Richards Foundation.*

Maxie Richards is an elderly lady with a compassion for drug addicts and those caught in the drugs epidemic. She allowed her house to be used as a detox centre for addicts and her Foundation helped thousands who used her small home as theirs. She wasn't immune to thefts and disappointments by her charges but still she carried on.

On one occasion she had several addicts living in her tiny two bedroom house. I loved the voluntary work I did for her taking her beloved "users" to dentists, HIV testing, the cinema and on the odd occasion, golf.

She stood for a seat in Parliament on the ticket of revealing the dangers of methadone. She warned that the policy to supply addicts with methadone would only increase the death rate from overdosing which had touched 400 that year. I canvassed for her along with a wee team of volunteers. Her words have come back to roost regarding the uselessness of methadone and a *Daily*

Record report from 2012 detailed the brave stance she made (see Appendix 1).

I can't speak highly enough of the lady.

Finishing the Adolphin building

Over the coming years I managed to get the Adolphin Building finished but not before the original owner took me to court for what was left of his outstanding payment of £2k.

It didn't matter to him that the house was on the market – he felt he had waited long enough. What came back from court was that the first £2k of any sale would be his. He was an old gent and although he gained no extra I think he enjoyed putting me, a Glasgow boy, in my place. I will however, always be grateful to him for the opportunity he gave me by selling the building. I will add a wee miracle into the renovation story for it shows me, on reflection, how my Saviour's hand was on me.

With money being tight, I decided to paint the gable end of the building myself. I was at the top of the 30 foot ladder with my paint pot attached by a hook and reaching to the side when I slipped and started to fall straight down.

It felt like slow motion as I thought silently, "Oh, no," being aware that each rung of the ladder was passing by quicker before my eyes the nearer I came to the ground.

On impact I literally bounced up into the air, still in slow motion before falling backwards and then finally landing squarely on my back. I decided to just lie there for a moment with the horrible thought that someone may have witnessed my trampoline exercise.

The fall only took a couple of seconds, as I lay on the ground knowing that I was okay I just felt comfortable knowing that I was in the Lord's hands. Needless to say, wisdom kicked in and I put the ladders and paint away for someone else to complete.

The King's Court

It was my original intention to turn *Adolphin Building* into a respite centre for addicts and their children with nursery and laundry facilities and to have courses for the parents while their children were being attended to.

My business plan was all sorted and further development of the site was drawn up by the architect. I put the building on the market after getting a £150k evaluation, and to my surprise I found out that Maxie was interested in buying it as a detox unit for her work.

At this time I went to a house group and during a quiet time in prayer I felt the Lord say, "The men that will use Adolphin Building will be used to being transported to the Police Court, the Sheriff Court and the High Court; call Adolphin Building the *'King's Court'* in my name."

And that's what I did and that's what it is called today, all for the glory of Jesus.

Now then, the sale had not gone through by this time and Maxie had met with Sir Lachlan McLean of the Robertson Trust that knew of Maxie's sterling work.

I sat in at the informal meeting at Maxie's house as Sir Lachlan laughed and said, "It's the first time we've been asked to fund something when the seller and the buyer are being interviewed at the same time."

Maxie's funding came through but one of her board felt a second survey would be in order and I had no objection to this as I had used a local surveyor myself.

To my dismay Maxie's board member came back with another quote from the same surveyor but this time it was for £100k.

I couldn't believe it and Maxie was distraught too. I called the surveyor and spoke to the young lad who had done the survey to ask how he had come to this price for the newly renovated six flats.

He informed me that it was all about his experience in the area and that was what he felt the house was worth.

I told him what I know he should have known, that it's all to do with square footage, if it was a new build, a derelict site or restored, and especially location of the site. He was obviously shocked when I interrupted his argument to say that I had it surveyed at £150k by a local firm.

Before he could get past the comment of, "It's all about perceptions, Mr Clark," I informed him that it was his Dad and his Dad's firm who had completed my survey months prior to his "price perceptions."

You could have heard a pin drop, even over the phone. When he got back to me Maxie had informed me that he had upped his survey to £130k.

Being under pressure to pay back my two debts I reluctantly agreed to the deal, besides it was Maxie who would have her desired rehab centre met.

So the King's Court was sold, I paid off the monies that I owed and booked up a holiday in Disneyland for Barclay and Brogan. My kids loved Disney – I came back a physical shell but a contented dad.

Heart by-pass

Allow me to interject by letting you know how I got on with my heart surgery. I was booked in at the Western Infirmary for a triple by-pass. I remember getting a bus to the top of Byres and walking slowly for twenty minutes to get to the hospital. I just wanted to get my head clear and to talk with my Lord Jesus.

By this time I was divorced and knew that the new girlfriend I had spent time with was not going to last. As I was booked in I was comfortable and at peace with what was about to happen.

I was first in line on the day for my operation and relaxed as I was put under by the anaesthetist. When I came around from the operation the pain was excruciating, not only to me but also the wee nurse who was wheeling me from the theatre and into the recovery room. Apparently I had come out of the anaesthetic too quickly and was attempting to pull at the tubes and cables that were going in and out of my body.

I could hear this wee angel saying in a concerned voice, "Oh Mr Clark, please don't, please don't touch the tubes."

She was struggling with me as I realised I was about to die with thirst rather than a heart by-pass. So I did a deal with her as I begged her for water, and as she was now assisted by another nurse, she agreed.

"There Mr Clark, I can't give you water but here try these," she exclaimed and put the best ice cube in the world into my mouth.

It was unusual to come out of the anaesthetic as quickly as I did but I did manage to get my wee angel to supply me with more frozen contraband.

My recovery was slow those first couple of days when they transferred me from Intensive Care into the high dependency ward. The pain was high and I was told that I was on maximum dosage by sympathetic staff who were at my beck and call.

My pastor, Alex Gillies, and his wife Charlotte came to see me, and almost left me for dead, well that was how it felt. Alex had passed me the bottle of cold water he had brought and by the time he left I had drunk a fair amount.

Within a few minutes it started. HICCUPS! "Oh no!" I shouted internally, in silent pain as I realised I should not have drunk carbonated water.

The staff were beside themselves with care to a point that the sister got the doctor to increase the dosage of morphine, however it had to be administered by another channel, but it worked.

I was finally transferred into a main ward. Being so drained and tired and not forgetting that I had lost a lot of weight, I was exhausted as I lay on this bed with three other patients in the ward for company. It's a clear memory I have as I remember what happened next.

Lying on my bed of pain with my eyes closed, I told the Lord I was worn out big time and that I had not slept properly for three days. Thanking Him for the comfort of the pain being reduced I asked Him to give me rest, I prayed for sleep.

As I finished that prayer I looked up at the clock and the second hand was approaching the hour mark, it was exactly eleven o'clock in the morning. Into a deep sleep I fell as comfort wrapped itself all around me, just before I realised that I was sitting on the edge of the earth's atmosphere.

With my legs comfortably crossed I could see the furthest planet and stars with a clarity that I can't explain. My life flashed through my mind missing nothing out; no fears or sorrows, no worries or pain, just a flashing through like a dry clean in a comfort zone that left no residue. Only one thing that was like a fly in the ointment was that I felt alone.

To my comfort, even to this day, I know my Saviour was there for He says in His word that He will *"never leave me nor forsake me"*.

This dream/vision seemed to happen in a place where there was no time and all I felt was complete rest and relaxation as I awoke. I was not shocked or surprised when I saw that the second hand on the clock was just leaving twenty seconds past eleven.

Yes, it was something special and it was from my Lord Jesus.

My body was rested and relaxed as comfort continued to work on the stresses of the previous days.

Having this amazing insight into the glories of the heavens I allowed myself to fall back into this place of peace knowing full well that I was going to experience the exact same thing again, which I did. The only difference this second time was that I just slept on and through it. By the time Saturday came I wanted home especially because Celtic were playing in a cup final. My specialist was reluctant but I assured him I would be fine.

"Fine you may be, Mr Clark, but your potassium levels are very low and I don't even know if you can walk up the hospital stairs next to the fire escape, never mind getting stressed out by a football match."

To which my nurse suggested, "Why don't you come back this way, doctor, and we can try Mr Clark on the stairs."

I had a couple of hours to get the potassium sorted, which was quickly done when my nurse stuffed a banana down my face. Standing on the fire escape landing with the doctor watching I managed to walk up and down as my new potassium figures showed that the levels had risen. Freedom and football! What a combination.

When I paid my yearly visit to a new heart specialist, I asked why I was still getting some angina pain. He went through my notes and said that the double by-pass I had, had been a success. I stopped him to let him know that it was triple by-pass I had undergone. He spent more time in his notes.

He hummed a bit and then informed me that I was right, that I had been scheduled for a triple by-pass but that the surgeon on duty had found one of the blockages in one artery was too close to the heart to attempt its bypass.

Asking him what artery was causing the problem, was it the 30 percent or the 60 percent or the 80 percent blocked one that had been left, he sat back for a second and asked me, "Are you a doctor, Mr Clark?" genuinely impressed with my medical acumen.

I was really pleased with myself before I "grassed" on my ego. "No doctor, that's what my last surgeon told me," I replied deflated as he went on to say, "It won't cause you too much bother, but if it does just use the spray you have."

And with that, I am once again indebted to the NHS.

Within a week I drove up to Inverness and spent another week convalescing in my mate John's house.

15

Carstairs

As I recuperated from my heart by-pass I got involved with Kilmarnock Prison as a prison visitor where we met one day per week to speak with the inmates. Following that Pastor Colin Cuthbert invited me to join him to go to Carstairs State Hospital.

On arrival we were taken to the high security wing to speak and play some music to the inmates. About eight patients were present but there was one man who looked familiar.

'Nobby's' journey

Each patient was heavily medicated but the one who caught my eye had a large tattoo on his forearm that said "IAN".

At the break I asked him what his name was and he said, "Nobby." "But it says 'IAN' on your arm," I replied. He looked at me, then he looked at the tattoo, before pointing to the ink stain that said "I" and moved his finger on to "A" and finished on "N" while spelling out **I Am Nobby.**

"A belter," I thought, "and he's the one in Carstairs."

"What's your second name?" I inquired, looking for any more telling tattoos.

"Clark," he said slowly. "Nobby Clark from Maryhill."

He was my father's cousin…my second cousin.

I had never heard about him but with the knowledge that he was family I spent the coming years attempting to get him downgraded from the high security facility where he was held. This quest did not happen at first as I had no intention of going against why he had been incarcerated, but as I learned more of his story I decided to take up his cause.

I visited Ian regularly and as I did he kept wanting to tell me that he should not have been sent to the unit he was in. I spoke to his psychiatrist, Dr Campbell, and told her that Ian was persistent in his attempt to tell me why he had been sent to Carstairs and that he had felt it was an injustice. What she said took me aback.

She told me that Ian should not be in any high security unit and that while he may cause harm to himself by missing his medication, he certainly was not a danger to the public.

With this information I began to listen to Ian's plight.

When he was sixteen he had been hit over the head with a golf club while he was a passenger on a scooter. He was left with brain trauma which led to a mental disability and this only complicated any diagnosis he would have in the future. Ian went on to tell me that when he felt bad he would sign himself into one of the hospitals as a volunteer out patient.

One night in the mixed wards, Ian and his girlfriend met in the toilets for whatever reason but his girlfriend, who was also a patient, had broken her ankle so she was in a wheelchair.

Two male nurses came in and ordered Ian back to his room but he refused. A struggle broke out and Ian was forcibly held down as an injection was administered. Ian kicked out and caught one of the male nurses in the face and in the melee his girlfriend was knocked over in her wheelchair.

Ian was put into a secure room and had not been released from that category over the fifteen years he had spent in Carstairs. I started to go to his monthly assessment meetings and every time his case came up there was always a comment like, "But we know what Ian has been like."

By persistence, and with Dr Campbell's input, we got Ian downgraded from the high security wing and into a regular locked ward. After a couple of years we managed to get him into Leverndale Hospital before he went on to Stobhill Hospital and then on to a hostel. It was a long road for a man called **I Am Nobby.**

Barclay and his guitar

As a prison visitor to HMP Kilmarnock, I got the opportunity on occasion to take Barclay along with me after we had him registered to visit.

My son loves his guitar and he writes Christian songs as he sings and plays his guitar. His strumming is excellent and his chord shapes are perfect, but he never gets the shapes on to the proper chords. So we have an enthusiastic young man who is tone deaf and loud, but loves every second of playing and singing music.

Barclay

On one of these prison visits we had a few musicians in to play for the inmates, including long term prisoners. Barclay was bursting to get up and sing with his guitar and was prompted by the pastor to join in. I stood with him in front of fifty inmates as he let rip trying to keep up with the song being played by the group. At the end of the chorus I put my hand out to get him to stop and was immediately told by the inmates to "Leave Barclay alone, let him play." I was delighted with this response from the men but not half as much as Barclay as he did his own solo encore to thunderous applause.

This reminds me of another time when I used to visit St Marks Church to have lunch with the homeless. We had our small service that included music, but Barclay wanted to preach. My son has another desire and that is to share God's Word.

Colin (the same prison pastor) said he could give a short word which delighted Barclay, meanwhile the sweat was running down my back. So I warned him not to take any longer than a few minutes.

At the interval, up he got with his bible, put it on the lectern and turned from page to page. This went on for a couple of minutes before I intervened to be told by him that it's alright.

A few minutes more and the company was getting restless as the bible pages were being turned this way and that. I once again got up and said, "What are you looking for?" Barclay stopped and looked at me as if I should know what the problem was before he said, "I'm looking for the beginning." Our meeting ended on a high and a laugh, but that's my son.

An invitation from Maxie

Maxie then approached me to see if I would be interested in managing her 5,000sq foot factory which she had obtained in Port Glasgow. I knew that her charity could not afford wages so I made an application for funding for two jobs regarding her furniture restoring factory.

The Foundation was successful and was granted a three year funding package for both myself and my friend John who was an upholsterer. No sooner was I in the job than I was asked if it was possible to run the Foundation's three shops along with the factory and all it entailed. This was something that I could get my teeth into. So along with John we decided to go for it.

The small factory had a load of damaged M&S furniture with old and new, scratched and dent damage goods all needing attention – it was stock destined for landfill.

With the new position I had taken on, John and I visited the M&S furniture manufacturers in Wales to purchase discontinued material that was going up for sale in their Welsh manufacturers' outlet. We managed to fill our van with all sorts of accessories along with pallets of materials. On the way out of the factory I noticed a mountain of rattan three piece suites through an open shed door. After speaking with our contact who was taking us around their factory we found it had been an over order that was stored in the hope of further sales.

I made them an offer and they agreed to it after I had phoned Maxie to get the all clear. The following week we had over 150 three piece rattan suites, included some damaged, that filled our small factory. These suites sustained us financially for the coming six months.

Justin and Colin – two famous Glasgow designers – came into our shop and bought one of the suites for a TV programme they fronted. They painted the suite and in their programme mentioned our shop. We were inundated with enquiries and the suites were sold in no time. It was then we decided to move into a larger factory that suited us down to a T.

My upholstery pal John felt he would just prefer to do his work at the factory so I took on the shops and distribution as well as overseeing the factory outlet alone. We had the lads from the *King's Court* coming in every day for John to teach along with a host of unemployed placements from the Port Glasgow area. I was busy travelling between the two outlets but I loved every minute of it. We worked hard for three years and managed to keep our profit margins high.

It became apparent that the £25k rental for the factory was going to be a burden once the initial funding for John and I stopped.

The *Maxie Richards Foundation* extended our contracts for another two years but it was to end in sorrow for myself. One of my major disappointments at Maxie's, besides the final outcome, was the unfinished vision I had for an old Dunkirk fishing boat.

I had kept in touch with Professor John Atkinson and to my delight he contacted me to see if we were interested in restoring a World War II Dunkirk boat. I was over the moon and we arranged free transport of the ship to our large Port Glasgow factory although we had to enlarge the doorway to get the *Resolute* into the factory. The boat was a disaster but it had a lot of items that could be restored, on the rebuild I intended including the engine which had been refurbished. We worked on it for a year but only on a cosmetic front as I was too busy building up the sales outlet for the Foundation.

It's a project I regret not having the time to pursue due to the circumstances that would unravel as the years passed.

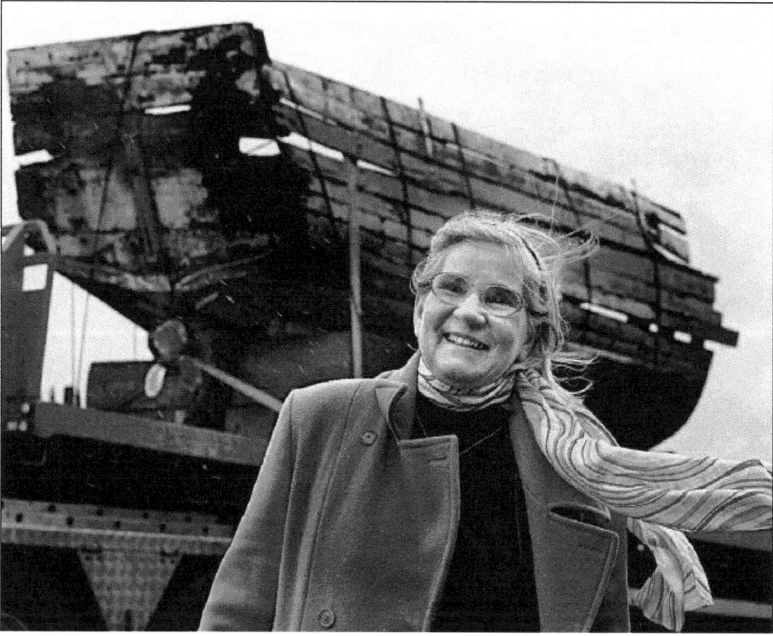

Two Heroines: Maxie Richards greets the remains of The Resolute as it arrives at her Foundation's workshop in Port Glasgow for restoration. It helped save lives at Dunkirk, now the Resolute is saving addicts. (Newspaper report at the time – see Appendix 2).

16

India

While working at Maxie Richards' Foundation I took time off to go to India with our church who had sponsored *Catherine Homes* orphanage in Andhra Pradesh, east India. Our church had been invited to visit the orphanage by its pastor Yesu Pedam. The orphanage also catered for widows who lived on site and this worked well for the children.

I took my daughter Brogan, who was now 16, along with me in the team of seven. She was so excited and had all her holiday clothing and make up well packed and ready for the journey.

Days before we were due to depart there was a terrorist attack on the Hotel Mumbai and we were given the option of pulling out of the trip, which we declined to do. When we arrived at Hyderabad Airport late at night we left the air conditioned and palatial settings to be picked up in the massive car park.

There was a sense of poverty as we drove towards our hotel. If the truth be told, I felt we had arrived in the middle of a refuse centre. The humid conditions did nothing to help the unpleasant aroma that impregnated the air as we drove to our destination in the dead of night.

On arriving at our hotel, two large metal gates opened and then closed behind us. We were once again surprised at the good condition of the hotel compared to the buildings and roads we had just driven through.

Next morning we decided to go out and onto the streets which seemed like a never ending market place. We were advised not to give out any money to beggars as there would be a chance we could be mobbed, so most of our team meandered down through the hustle and bustle of Hyderabad.

One of our team, Al, could not help but feel compassion for a young girl holding a baby in an old, tattered shawl. When she repeatedly put her five fingers towards her mouth in a "needing food" gesture, his heart just gave way to the advice we had been given. No sooner had the young girl received Al's generous gift than a crowd rushed out and encircled us. Brogan got the fright of her life as I felt her grab me with all her might. I don't know what happened but all I can remember is shouting out at the top of my voice which forced the group of beggars to recoil.

I, for one, could feel my Lord's protection from a situation that could have got out of hand. Once we got safely back to the hotel we joked about the rush of Indians that encircled us. "They obviously didn't know we are from Glasgow," was one of the light hearted comments.

Brogan was shocked as she realised that this holiday was not going to be like any other she had had. In fact when we got to our destination, after another eight hour train trip, she told me she wanted to go home. As we settled into our rooms at the orphanage, however, things started to change as we were saturated by the love of the Indian people with a humility that is their strength.

Brogan and I shared a room and at night I was plagued by mosquito bites while Brogan was bite free.

We had a resident gecko that she was not fond of but I was determined to keep it in the house and was going to advertise to see if any of its family wanted to join us. It was the only way I could think of reducing the blood I was losing to the mosquitos each night. Once Brogan got to meet the orphans then things changed quickly as I saw a genuine compassion rise from deep within her, so much so that even today she desires to return.

One day we spoke to one of the orphanage staff who was the brother-in-law of Pastor Yesu Pedam. He told us that he was actually a teacher but worked at the orphanage as a handyman/security employee. He went on to say that he had two children that were ill and asked us to pray for them. A lot of illnesses come from the contaminated water that the locals drink. This seemed to be a general problem for the whole of Andhra Pradesh and bottled water was the only safe way to drink water.

When I started *Open Gates,* this situation came to mind which is why we help communities with drinking water and have included that aim in our charity's constitution.

None of us, including the orphans, were allowed to leave the compound alone; we always needed to be accompanied for safety's sake.

We were told that a few months prior to our visit a small Christian church in a jungle area, not too far from the orphanage, had been attacked. The congregation had been locked in their building with a chain padlocked on the outside of the church door. As the attackers, who were Hindu Fundamentalists, were about to set the building on fire, an army patrol vehicle passed and rescued the congregation. We actually paid two visits to the small building in question.

Each night we went to a village to preach and share the Word of God and on one particular night I had a wee accident much to the hilarity of all who witnessed it. As I bade my farewell I was walking backwards while waving to a sea of smiling faces when, to the horror of the onlookers, my right leg disappeared into a pit of liquefied cow dung. I did not get the chance to sink further than my knee before a dozen hands pulled me free. Commotion followed as containers of water were poured over my soiled leg like a tsunami. All I could hear above the din was the pastor's wife in fits of laughter which caught on more and more the cleaner my leg became. All I lost that night was a bit of pride and a good shoe that never again matched my unsoiled one.

By the time our visit at the orphanage ended we were blessed by the work carried out by a pastor who has a deep desire to look after orphans and widows. Brogan has such a conviction and desire to return and I pray that her heart's desire is met. Our church has managed to build a large bible college there – Paul Gillies Bible College – that is being used to this day.

Back at the factory – Fred and Lawrie

In any business I have had, or employment I've secured, job satisfaction has always been a serious factor for me. Yes, it's good to get a fair wage, but job satisfaction is the icing on the cake for me. I have never spent any great length of time in a job that I didn't enjoy.

Fred was an elderly gent who knew how to set up a fully operational machine shop. His stories became the main topic every lunch time (probably because we could not get a word in) as he would go into the tiniest detail, much to the lads' interest and amusement.

As our factory was very long, it took a fair step out to get from one end to the other. One day, I heard Fred coming from a distant section of the factory shouting, "Get an ambulance, he's in a bad way!"

When he got to me he dropped his voice and breathlessly said, "I think we have lost him Pat, the wardrobe fell on his head." I looked around to see if anyone was about, but not one person was in sight as I ran towards the top end of the factory.

In among our wardrobes I saw that one of them was lying on the ground with someone underneath. It was an old Victorian mahogany wardrobe and the body was trapped in such a way that his head and part of his shoulder were wedged under its full weight. All I could see were his overalls and a glove on the free hand, I looked towards his boots just to see if I could recognise who it was.

As I got nearer the body I was sure that one of the legs was broken by the angle it lay at. Fred was a bit behind me when I stood over the corpse and realised that it was a dummy so well dressed and laid out by some of our guys who now appeared from hidden positions with belly aches of laughter. Only one person was upset and I don't think we ever managed to get Fred to see the funny side of it, which made it even funnier.

Now, you might think you would not have been duped by such a silly prank, but that is because you don't know Lawrie.

Lawrie was one of the most skilled men I have had the pleasure of working with. From restoration to sign writing he had it together as he had been a stage manager for the *Pavilion Theatre* in Glasgow. His experience and knowledge were invaluable and his sense of fun was unmatched in the precision he set up any unsuspecting victim.

A valuable art find?

I have had the pleasure of meeting Peter Howson the artist, through Walter Souter (board member and friend) and I quite liked his work. Walter got me a couple of signed prints and I had a brochure of all his works in my desk.

One of the men came into the office one day and asked if I could help him with a piece of furniture I had brought and was due for restoration. "We just cannot get it open Pat, we have all had a try and I need to get the drawer out before I can get it refurbished," came the excuse from one of our younger team.

I was a bit annoyed as I looked towards Will, who was a volunteer and sat at the other desk in the office. As I reluctantly made my way to the chest of drawers, Will was in my wake. Four or five men were in the area looking over towards the offending piece of furniture, which did not help alleviate my mood.

"Get out the way," I said to no one in particular trying to keep my voice jocular. I placed my feet solidly against the drawer's base and yanked it out with not too much force. Yes, it was a bit tight but I was quite happy to take any plaudits that were going as I heard from somewhere in the background, "I told you Pat would have got it."

As I was walking away with much pride and with Will in attendance, I noticed that under the paper that lined the drawer was a sketched drawing. I pulled it out and recognised it as a Howson drawing, much to my delight.

"Do you know what this is?" I asked as I waved it above my head like a trophy. "It's a Howson!" I exclaimed triumphantly to anybody who wanted to listen. Comments of, "Aye, right," and, "No, it isny," were closed down by me telling them to come to the office and I would show them the exact sketch in the Howson brochure I had in the office.

Sure enough, I had some of the guys follow me as I got out Mr Howson's book of art to show them the exact sketch that I now held in my hand. They really did not have to tell me but Lawrie had got his full "wind up" completed when he told me to look at the back of the sketch I had just found. It was a drawing done on a piece of binned paper that had an old email of mine printed on the back.

Lawrie had come in that morning, looked at the Peter Howson catalogue and had forged the drawing before he got a sponge with tea on it and wiped it to make it look that bit older. He then said to me, "Look at the date Pat, if Peter Howson had done that on the date I have written he would only have been four years old."

Now that was run of the mill for pranks and wind ups, but even as I was being told this by Lawrie, Will was still on the phone trying to price and authenticate the catalogue sketch that was in our possession.

Heartbreak Hotel

I had planned to remarry and agreed with my girlfriend's wish to buy a hotel in the Glendaruel area, in Argyll and Bute, after we were engaged. She was a lady that I had employed at Maxie's shop. Sadly, things did not work out between us and with the hotel. It was a period of great pain and disappointment and, as she was also employed in Maxie's Foundation at the shop, things spilled over into my work situation.

The end result was that I left the Foundation and in the course of events I lost some precious friendships. I also had to sell my house to repay mortgage debts related to the hotel and became unemployed.

It had been a great privilege to have worked for the Foundation but it was time to move on and the experience led to me setting up *Open Gates*.

It also gave me the experience of depending on the Lord for future trials that lay ahead as there were more still to come. My pastor, Alex Gillies, and his wife Charlotte were pillars of strength to me during this time. And by the grace of God I came through it, and through His word which comforted and directed me through the mental storm. A wee poem that I wrote years prior did help:

How Come I Am So Low This Day?

How come I am so low this day
Doing things wrong and not the right way?
Not just paddling, but swimming in the depths of despair
When there's absolutely no reason for me to be there.
I tell my spirit to rejoice – even to respond.

233

You see, I have a Saviour and we have a bond.
So what way can I be worthy, what way can I be true?
Not only submitting to Him but also submitting to you?

Each time when the pressure got too much I would just sit and read a scripture over and over or recite the poem. It was better than any medication on the market. After I got through those years I could say that I can forgive my former girlfriend while at the same time asking to be forgiven. I have no animosity whatsoever towards my ex-partner.

17

Open Gates

Egg on Your Face or a Word From God?

A strange heading for a word of revelation I suppose, but my wee story of *Open Gates* comes under the above category. The original vision started around 1995. I owned the sandwich business that saw me travelling about the country in my attempt to boost sales. It was well after 4pm on a lovely sunny afternoon when I drove over the Cathkin Braes, a hilly area on the outskirts of Glasgow, on my way back to my west end factory in Drumchapel.

As I looked to my right I caught the lovely sight of Glasgow's north side of the city that sat below the hill top I was driving on. From my position, with the Campsie hills in the background, I was captivated. It seemed so beautiful that I felt compelled to pull onto the side of the road and get out of my car to look down on the city. This was unusual for me, for while I enjoy scenery

– I was brought up going to a school that faced the same Campsie Hills – I can take or leave "beauty sights".

So what was it that had stopped me and to stand at the side of a main road with cars passing in both directions and stare at this Scottish scenery?

I got out of the car, I walked around to the passenger side where I placed my folded arms on the roof. Resting my chin on the back of my hands I knew that this scenery was special, this time was special.

With the rolling Campsie Hills as a backdrop and a clear sunny sky as a ceiling of a blue, there was one low levelled cloud that spoiled the perfection of this wonderful picture. The cloud itself was imposing and I think it may have been this that first caught my attention.

I heard nothing from the passing cars that zipped by in front of me in both directions as I studied the cloud. It was large, but from my high viewpoint at eye level I could see the top as well as the bottom of the grey and black cigar shaped cloud.

Under the dark shadow, which gave me a strange feeling, the north part of the city looked as if it was dull, dank and grey – like an old unwanted fading tattoo. The dark shadow covered the north side of the city of Glasgow. Under this canopy everything seemed so sterile and sad. On such a beautiful night, this cloud had the make-up to stop the pleasant evening sunlight from reaching the land and its people.

The colours of blue from the sky, orange from the setting sun and the brown/green of the Campsie Hills held no detraction from the many silver rays of light that began to burst through the thick cloud with laser beam precision.

All at once, like a large circular searchlight, one main silver beam arrowed on to the ground and covered the central part of the clouds shadow with bright silver light. The light itself seemed brighter than sunlight; it was certainly a different colour. I don't know how long I stood there for, but I was not in a rush to leave. I was still not aware of the traffic and the people that were passing in their cars. They had not seen, or were even aware, of what I was witnessing. How were they to know that this large searchlight was shining on an area that I knew well.

I also felt that this was a sign from the Lord, and the first thought that came to my mind was, "light in a dark place." I had such a feeling of excitement and peace, both in equal measure and at the same time, which overwhelmed and complemented the strange feeling I was having.

As I drove back into Glasgow I was sure I had a word from the Lord for our church. The church I attended was in Possil and it seemed to stand almost in the centre of the main beam of silver light I had just witnessed. I was sure that the Lord was showing me that revival was going to come in the Possil area where the light had shone. I could not wait to get home and when I did I drew a picture of what I had seen on an acetate.

Open Gates: The vision starts to take shape

I was attending Possil Christian Fellowship at Elsmere Street, Possil, Glasgow for just over one year which is an area with a high percentage of folk with addictions and convictions.

In that first year I had settled well but had not made a heartfelt commitment to the fellowship although I was attending and taking part in all the meetings and gatherings. At that time I also met Colin Cuthbert who had started and was running *Prison Fellowship* from one of the church's offices.

So my time there was great but I felt that my loyalty to my old fellowship, New Life Christian Centre, had not subsided enough for me to "fully" commit to the Possil church, even though my old fellowship had ceased to exist.

Sharing

So there I was, talking enthusiastically to my new pastor and explaining that revival – which we had all been praying for – was coming to Possil, and that I had had a sign to prove it.

He smiled and said, "Okay Pat, on you go, share it with the church." Now then, not being the shy type was a bit different from putting your faith on the line. Putting your faith on the line is fine, but to share it out in front of the congregation was a step further than that.

I can't remember what went through my mind at the time, I just went up in front of the church and shared what I felt the Lord had shown me, acetate and all. I informed them that the Lord's light was shining in our area and that our church stood at the centre of the light I had seen.

I think my revelation and prophetic utterance went okay and I felt I had done what I was supposed to do. I had shared what I had seen and boldly said what I knew the Lord was saying. It also felt good to unload this "Word from God" for others to pick up. Obedience is the factor to His prompting.

A few weeks later the pastor announced that he and his family were committing themselves to the fellowship for the forthcoming four years. That gave me a chance to go to him and say that my family and I would do the same and I fully committed my family to the Possil Fellowship.

So there I was happy and contented, worshipping the Lord, getting to know about all at *Prison Fellowship*, the *Drop In* and their ministries.

Things changed a few weeks later when the pastor announced that something had come up and he was resigning from our fellowship to take up a new post. He fully explained his situation and left us with our blessing.

So there I was convincing myself that the vision was not about any one person, it was about what the Lord was going to do in this area that I worshipped in, even if I was not involved (well that was the explanation I gave myself).

Not long after this the Possil Fellowship had a couple of new pastors before the building was then passed over to *Emmaus* for a homeless unit. I am now a member of Victory Christian Centre, Govan, Glasgow, AoG, whose pastor is Alex Gillies.

So my faith, although a bit dented and wobbly on the prophetic side, (I actually felt I had spiritual egg on my face) was still as strong in our Lord Jesus.

Emmaus, in turn, redeveloped the church site and now use it to restore damaged furniture as well as accommodation for their homeless clients, and doing a good job too.

The Lord 'opens doors'

I have given you my testimony about our Lord Jesus and the way that He drew me to Himself in 1983 after years in and out of prison.

Following that I have been in business most of my life and always been blessed to choose and do work that I liked. My last job was working for a charity that dealt with addictions and for five years I was a Sales and Marketing manager and ran three shops and a factory where we had a number of furniture restoration projects on the go.

As my work contract was ended I was approached by one of the senior volunteers who confronted me with a serious face when he said, "You can't stop doing this, and you need to start this going again."

I think that was the third time I had heard that same word that week and it had lined up with a word and a written note I had received from my dear brother, Jacky Lynch, who is a member of the same church. Jacky had come to me in March 2010 and said that the Lord was going to use me "to 'open doors' that could not be opened and 'close doors' that could not be closed."

Anyway, I knew that the Lord was speaking to me and in prayer I put it before Him. If I was to do this I needed a factory. I knew that most of the volunteers I had worked with would be delighted to come along with a new venture.

This was the beginning of the venture and how God led me to start *Open Gates*.

The 'egg' disappears with a revelation!

My dear friend, Marion, and members at Harvest Christian Fellowship Hamilton (AoG) called me to a prayer meeting in a couple, Ellen and Jack's house. They felt Our Lord was calling them to prayer for *Open Gates*. I was asked at the prayer time, "Pat, what is your vision for *Open Gates*?"

I kind of stammered and said, "Well, the Lord convinced me and laid it on my heart to do this. With confirmation coming from Jack's word at church, and my fleece for a factory…" Before I could finish Ellen interrupted, "No Pat, what is your vision for *Open Gates*?"

It was then that the "spiritual egg" on my face was wiped away by revelation. The acetate I drew my vision on, so that I could show the saints at the Possil Church, had been misplaced, but I remembered from my drawing the silver lights that shone from that dark cloud onto the Possil area covered the factory that we now lease.

Adding to this the Scottish Canals Offices (who agreed to give us the factory and is our landlord) lie beside the old Possil Church; its car park wall is shared with the church (which is now *Emmaus*) I used to attend. So between the church, the Scottish Canals Office and our factory lies about 500 yards of a distance – yet it was 17 years of a waiting to get there.

18

Open Gates 2010: Beginnings

I had finally managed to find out who owned a derelict factory I had seen at Dawson Road, I also had two other properties to view.

The Herschel Street building in Anniesland was ready to move into and the old Bellahouston Academy, with large rooms on two floors, was offered along with a car park. The Bellahouston Victorian building was beautiful and all I had to do was sign up to a lease with a three month free rent period.

The day I got in to the old Pars Bakery at Dawson Road, however, (which was leased to Scottish Canals) I knew that this was the place I was to set down the roots for *Open Gates*. Herschel Street and Bellahouston Academy had no chance.

Don't forget I was planning this with faith for I had no money for this venture…I just believed.

The first time I met with their manager Marcus Kroner, the Scottish Canals Estate Manager, to view the premises we could not get into the factory as there had been a bit of a dispute with some of the local scrap vultures. These guys had changed the locks on the gates and doors as they systematically stripped the building of its internal metals – stainless steel, copper wire, and aluminium were all on their shopping list along with a cast iron boiler and four ovens.

As Marcus apologised, he left me with the promise he would get the locks fixed and meet me back at the factory in a few days. As he left, I just walked around the front of the building feeling that this was the right location for my vision.

While meditating on this, I was startled when a window's roller shutter opened with a clatter and two men sprung out.

"What are you doing hanging about here?" came a question that was really a challenge.

"Moving into this factory I have just got," I bluffed being just as confrontational as they were before challenging them by saying, "And what are you two doing here?"

Just to save time, I followed this up by immediately asking the question in the same aggressive tone. "Where do you two come from?" I was hoping it was local, which it was, to my delight.

So I told them my name and who my relatives were and that was the password that allowed me through their security system.

They then invited me in through the window and closed the shutter behind us. They were the last batch of metal prospectors and were cleaning up any scrap that had not already been removed.

"Can you give us another day, we are nearly done, Pat?" one said pointing in the direction of the large oven carcass that stood derelict in a dark corner. It was obvious to me that if I got the building then I would need to remove what was left anyway.

I then came clean and told them that I was meeting the owners in a few days and it really wasn't my call. I left both of them hammering and cutting with all their might at what was left of their day's work. The thought did run through my mind that in the future they just might be two of our future service users.

When I met Marcus he had had his men change the locks so that allowed me to officially inspect the place. I told him of my encounter with two of his squatters and he informed me that they were fed up of changing the locks and he listened as I told him that the roof would be the next thing to go.

Now before I tell you what we saw as we entered I need to give you a bit of background regarding the old bakery.

It had been closed for a number of years and then leased out to a gentleman who manufactured dog and cat food. There was a stream of public complaints regarding the smell coming from the ovens he was using to cook the meats, which he sourced from meat market carcases. This manufacturer was forced to put a massive extractor on the roof with a door that had a dozen large filters to cut out the smells.

At the time I was not aware of the roof extractor that was jammed shut with solidified fat from cooking the pet food. Neither was I aware that when he was cooking the full carcases, the fats from the meats and the marrow from the bones ran into a trap that overflowed into the drainage system.

It took me a number of days to break down and dismantle the roof extractor and it was over five years before we finally had a full drainage system operational – but they were only the hidden problems.

The smell of the factory was bad and I was shown one of the rooms that held about one hundred large plastic bags containing fats that had had to be treated by Scottish Canals before they could be considered for disposal. Even though this treatment had been done, it did not lend itself to any "clean aromas" in the airwaves for the nostrils.

Marcus told me that the last tenant had just up and left and they had not found out about it for months. When they finally gained access the place was alive with maggots as well as residential rats.

I hope I have given you a back drop of the underlying work that needed sorted out because when we finally got to the car park door, three scaffolding planks had been laid on the internal floor, thus jamming against the door stopping anyone going in, probably placed there by the first set of tomb robbers.

The factory

Walking through the corridor to the main factory, we stood on those same scaffolding planks using it as our walkway which kept our feet dry. Entering into the main hall I could see the stripped ovens in the corner, but the floor was covered in heavy ceiling tiles that had fallen down.

The ground itself was sodden and the installation from the ovens was scattered all around the large room.

Electrical wiring had been stripped out from the main boxes to the switches. The toilets and basins had been smashed or cracked. There was a small boiler room where the aluminium roof had been damaged along with a wall that had housed the boiler. In their attempt to remove the small boiler, the thieves had abandoned their labours with the fear of bringing the whole roof down. The toilet extraction flues had been ripped from the ceilings and doors were damaged or missing.

It would take one hundred, one ton sacks of refuse to clear the main floor in this area alone.

The upper storey was not as bad only because there were less things to damage. But all the walls were punctuated and ripped open as stainless steel pipes and electrical wiring was stripped and removed.

At the rear of the building over one hundred wooden pallets were so rotten that we burned them on site. All external windows had iron sheets just to protect the glass (alas, all the glass had been broken from the inside.)

A massive gas tank had to be removed from the car park along with a barbed wire fence that was a danger to the public. The outer wall was in a dangerous state as was the entrance canopy on the gable of the building.

I hope this gives you a slight picture of what lay in store. Let me apologise for going on a bit but I want you to understand that that is not what I saw as I moved from floor to floor and room to room…instead I saw each space as a finished article, and each problem as a project.

Inspiration from Nehemiah

Logging all the work in my mind my first thought was to secure a lease from Scottish Canals (this was done one week later at £1 peppercorn rental per year). I do need to say that Nehemiah was on my mind and in prayers for I knew that he had rebuilt the walls of Jerusalem in fifty two days even though he had local opposition.

My priority now was to get the floor space cleared, get the pallets and barbed wire sorted along with the metal curtains that covered our windows. That was it.

It took me, along with my American friend Will, a Lithuanian visitor called Gintaras and a number of other volunteers, one year to shovel up and remove over one hundred ton sacks of debris, yes I did count them, into land fill.

Burning the pallets and cementing the vast hole in the floor that the ovens had been built into was our only goal for that first year. Having no money I made a deal with a scrap man I got to know. He could have all the scrap that was left on the condition that he took our rubbish to land fill. Done deal.

Gintaras moved into my home pending his application for a house. He had decided to live in Glasgow as he had some family living in the Govan area. He was a God send to me in those early months and years.

While we did have friends on hand that helped, Gintaras committed himself to the vision that I shared with him and he worked just as if it was his own purpose in life.

I had approached some friends in the church to join my board and decided to register the Charity on December 2010 with our constitution completed on 2011.

A miraculous £5 note

In 2013, while working in the factory, I was left with no option but to sell my house at a giveaway price just to meet the bank's demand regarding the loan for the hotel I had taken a few years previously. After the sale I had only enough money to pay my lawyer's fee. He in turn invited me for a coffee with his assistant, which was a big surprise to both of us, as he would not give you a nod if he was a rocking horse.

"You know I'm pratted Malcolm," I stated to reinforce his knowledge regarding my financial state.

"No problem, I'm paying," he bragged as we ordered our expensive lattes in the city's top coffee establishment.

"So, tell me Pat," he asked as he stirred his coffee. "You say that the Lord talks to you. Is that right?"

"Aye, He does Malcolm, in different ways," I replied as I noticed that his young assistant was smiling at me, for she too was a believer. "And what ways does He do that?" he inquired with more than a hint of unbelief on his face.

"All different ways, Malcolm – just a thought, just a coincidence, just a prayer. He does it in so many ways," I replied to a man whose dad was a minister. Going into how I became a Christian is something I like to share, so witnessing to my lawyer was, and is what I like and what I do.

It was then that he reverted back to type when he hit me with an order of, "Right, it's your turn. I'll have the same again and I'm sure my assistant will have the same." It was an order rather than a request. The young assistant reached over and touched my arm, "Not for me Pat, I'm fine," she said with a knowing smile.

She knew that her boss had just wiped out my financial stability with the bill I had just paid him. We had joked that my bill was exactly what had been remaining from the sale of the house. "Okay," I thought, "only one coffee to get," as I joined the long lunch time queue. Going through my pockets I found that I was one penny short in the change I had and with my last £10 note in my wallet, and I was not going to break that (an old habit from my Ma) for an expensive coffee.

When I got to the counter there was a large "tips" bowl filled to the top with money. I apologised to the girl for being a penny short.

"That's no problem, sir," she said with a large grin while taking a penny from the "tips" bowl and putting it in the till to cover my shortfall.

As I was walking down to the lower floor where my lawyer was seated I realised that I had forgotten his sugar. I turned and went back up to the service island at the top of the stairway. A bowl similar to the "tips" bowl held the sachets of sugars. I picked up three portions, two were square and one was pencil shaped.

Getting back to my two legal beagles I noticed that the pencilled shaped sugar was not sugar. As I put down the coffee, I un-wrapped the pencil shaped paper and found it to be a £5 note which had a small green note attached that said, *"A wee gift for* **you** *spend and enjoy."*

The first reaction from my lawyer was one of amazement as his assistant laughed out loud, before he said, "Aye right, you must have done that." But he knew that the words I had shared before going for his coffee had been confirmed and so did his assistant.

God's faithfulness and goodness brought me through that time and it was amazing to see how He showed His love so practically to me.

A photo of the actual fiver

From homeless to a new home

Moving quickly on and into my homeless situation. Having had to sell my house I was made homeless and becoming homeless meant that I was a priority for a house and that storage had been arranged for my furniture.

An appointment was made for me to book into a hostel for older men that would suit me while a house could be arranged for me to stay. The hostel was in the east end of Glasgow. The stay would only be for a couple of weeks at the most.

On the evening before I left my home I started to pack up odds and bobs when my phone rang. It was the couple who had just bought my house. They inquired if I would consider selling my living room sofas. I don't know why, probably because of all the hassle, but I asked if they were really interested to come and see me. After saying there was a bargain to be had both appeared within the hour.

They jumped at the chance when I offered them everything in my home for one thousand pounds. I meant everything, from my sofas to beds to white goods and even my golf clubs and snooker cue. So next morning all I had was a couple of cases of clothes and a hostel to go and see.

When I got to the hostel that night it was obvious to me that I could not stay, and my half-finished office in the factory was more suitable instead. Margaret, my ex-wife, got to hear about this and offered me her spare room for a couple of nights which was gratefully accepted. By the end of the week I had been given a temporary high rise flat. I settled in straight away and after six weeks, I was offered a small flat in the Yoker district.

I had peace all through this period especially when Barclay came to stay with me at the weekends in the high rise flat. During this whole event my work at the factory didn't stop.

Boots and dry bones

The first recollection that comes to mind that does not include factory renovation work was when my cousin Robert (another scrap man) came in to see us.

Now don't forget that there was no electricity in the building which meant that even during the day it was always dull. Robert came in with bags of working boots that he said came from another charity that he knew. This charity had closed and the boots were on offer to anyone who could use them.

So in they came in black bags, but it wasn't until later that we realised the boots had been worn. Gintaras and I just looked at one another and laughed. The thought of Ezekiel 37 and the *"dry bones"* came to my mind, so Gintaras and I placed the twenty three pairs of boots all in a row up against the wall. We then prayed workers, volunteers and service users into those boots.

19

Abraham's Wells

When in the bible we read the story in Genesis 26 of Isaac digging up his father Abraham's wells, he named them: *Sitnah* – Accusation; *Esek* – Argument; and *Rehoboth* – Roomy.

I went through all three experiences in the early years of the setting up and developing *Open Gates*. Along the way there were changes made to the way the charity was structured and in the personnel. And finally, after coming through that period – which took a number of years – I had a deep peace, and the enjoyment of going into the factory every day returned.

Every single person that has come through *Open Gates* has helped in the renovation of a badly run down building which is used for the benefit and welfare of others. My gratitude to everyone is sincere. Now we are in a situation where our charity is more than "roomy" for everyone.

The Team

While we were building *Open Gates* we had some great people who joined us on the journey.

Jim Cavana

Jim Cavana was a man I recognised, but didn't know from where. As I have said, I was a prison volunteer as well as a volunteer for the homeless at St Mark's in Possil where he too volunteered. We had met in the 90s through Prison Ministries which was started by Colin Cuthbert

I got to know Jim a lot better after we went to Atlanta to visit the local prisons. We both became a part of COPE (Coalition of Prison Evangelists) and were invited to share our testimony at Richmond Prison, Augusta.

COPE is a group of ex-cons who fund religious teachings in USA prisons, due to the cut backs in Christian prison ministry funding. This group had been involved with organised crime before they became Christians to then become sponsor preachers as well as prison visitors.

Jim had been a prison officer in Barlinnie. He was a slim healthy and fit man and although I did not have any personal dealings with him in prison I recognised him to be a fair man.

Jim had taken a brain seizure and was rushed into hospital for an emergency operation that saved his life. Unfortunately he was not able to work again, but still spent his every spare hour serving ex-offenders as well as encouraging those still in prison.

He was a soft spoken man with a good sense of humour and a faithfulness that stood him proud. The reason I mention Jim is that we both had a desire to see men stop habitually offending, yet we had come from two different sides of the fence.

I loved to be in his company and we were quick to inform prisoners and offenders that he used to be a Barlinnie Labourer, and I was his way of earning a living. They in turn, just like me, had a great affection for him. We lost Jim due to his ongoing state of health which caught up with him. He was sorely missed.

John and Davy

John, my upholsterer friend from Maxie's, had left the Foundation when it had closed. He had all his equipment and furniture put into storage in the Greenock area. We had a meeting and I agreed that he could use the factory to keep all his equipment on the understanding that he would train and teach our service users in upholstery and furniture restoration as well as restoring goods that we may get.

He was a great help in those early days along with a long term prisoner, Davy, who had been released years earlier.

Making progress and meeting a mentor

So we plodded away and managed to secure an agreement with the CPO (Community Payback Orders) once they had checked all our policies. I also had a meeting in Barlinnie to see if we would take in their long term prisoners (National Top End NTE) on placement. This we agreed to as well. We managed to get a £10k grant from the *Lottery* which allowed us to reinstate the electricity and water.

At the same time Walter Souter, who was a board member and friend, secured pallets of gyproc for a stud partitioning around all our tiled walls in the main hall at the factory.

The stud frames were erected and installed by my brother John. So we made considerable progress in those first couple of years. At the same time I was awarded an entrepreneurial grant of £5k with an add on. The add on was that I had to agree to be sponsored by a mentor. Mentor? Who me?

What did I need a mentor for? I knew everything, aye right.

That was my first reaction, but when Simon Brennan walked into my damp office with the small streams of condensation running down the tiled walls, I knew I was on a winner.

He had brought in four of the best scones I had seen in a long while. Now I don't know if that influenced me but it certainly helped. Simon was to come for one year, which he did religiously and he has ended up being with us ever since.

Going on eight years he is still my reins, and with baby steps systems he stops my galloping into any cul-de-sac. I do need to say that after his tenure was officially finished he was awarded the *Mentor of the Year* in the Glasgow City Halls. He's still my mentor but better than that, he is my friend.

Walter

It's worth bringing in Walter Souter's input as it was as important as any other member or volunteer, but to me he was more than that. I really don't know how he enjoyed my company for although he was short on words, his point always came across, usually aimed at me with a shake of the head.

He had put early lighting into the factory that allowed us to work clearer and safer. He came in one day with his van (he was an electrician) and Gintaras and I thought, "That's great, another pair of hands."

He opened the back doors and brought in four chairs that were destined for the dump and said, "Can't help you lads but these chairs will keep your clothes dry and off the floor," and with that he left, much to our amusement.

He went to our church and was not slow to tell Pastor Alex when he had overstepped his time preaching. I can't say enough about Walter and his support to myself and to *Open Gates*. He looked for nothing but gave his all. We lost him to pancreatic cancer, and I remember the day so well when Marion, a close friend, and I visited him. He had not received his test results but he knew that there was something seriously wrong.

At crucial points for *Open Gates* he encouraged me at a time when I should have been encouraging him.

On one occasion, I had once again succeeded in securing another £15k entrepreneurial grant in Edinburgh from *First Port*.

But I had come back to Glasgow really low because of challenges I was facing.

I drove straight to Walter's house and sat down with him and told him I was in an uphill struggle with some issues that were going on. I needed his advice, and Walter being Walter, replied, "If you chuck this, you are letting a lot of folk down," and with that he got up and went into the kitchen. Believe it or not it was a boost for me knowing that he wanted me to keep going. Six weeks before he died, he came to the factory and told me to inform the board that he was resigning because of his health.

I am pleased to say that the board rejected his resignation and when I went to tell him he laughed for ages and shouted to his wife, "Hey Ann, listen to this, they won't let me resign."

The "White House" project

While working away with the factory renovation I had been approached by Allan Davidson of the Glasgow Regeneration Department and he informed us that the "White House" pub on Maryhill Road was derelict and was owned by Scottish Canals, and asked if we would be interested in renovating it.

After a meeting with Scottish Canals we were designated to restore the oldest pub in the Maryhill area. This renovation was done to the highest standard and it is now run by another charity that pays and contributes rent into Scottish Canals.

We used four long term prisoners as our main work source in the renovation which complimented our tradesmen. This work was carried out while we were still upgrading our own factory.

Mart and Brian – rivals!

Mart walked through the factory door with a scowl on his face. "Can I speak to you Pat?" was the first thing he said to me on his first day of placement, as he ushered me into my own office.

I had been contacted by the Long Term prisoner authorities (NTE) to see if I was willing to take another placement to complement the two men I already had on site.

It had been explained to me that the man in question had such a reputation that every time he got a placement the prison authorities were inundated with complaints from the public. The public complaints were actually from this man's enemies.

Now when I was told he desperately needed a placement so as to trigger a release date, I accepted him immediately. I had known Mart in my past life, so a placement for him held no problems for me.

What I didn't know was that Big Brian (our first long term placement along with John the "Brush") and he were arch enemies in Barlinnie.

I closed the office door and Mart said, "Thanks for giving me this chance, it was my last hope, but before I start here you need to get rid of that big rat Brian." He then went on to say why he disliked him and that I would be better off getting rid of him.

As I let him continue his wee rant I had decided how I was going to deal with this jail talk.

"Okay Mart, I hear what you are saying," I said, "and what you are making clear is that you cannot work with big Brian. So now you have a choice, firstly, you can put your jacket on and I will take you back to Barlinnie, or you can get your act together, because I am not going to manage a two gang system at *Open Gates*."

He seemed taken aback by this as I continued, "Knowing you Mart, then it is better to perhaps get yourself back to Barlinnie and look for another placement."

He was flummoxed and said that he could not get another placement so he would just have to grin and bear it.

"Sorry Mart," I said, "that's not good enough for me as I need to see what Brian thinks about your placement as he has been here a while and has proved himself."

Suddenly my new placement was not so sure of himself.

I then spoke to Brian separately and asked him for his feelings about Mart coming on board. Brian was very much up front (he had told me that he had worked for me at Rolls Royale when he was a sixteen year old). When I said that if he could not deal with it I would let Mart go and get another placement this is what Brian's response was, "Listen Pat, I am not scared of him, and that is why he hates me. I don't care one way or the other if he stays or not."

I interrupted Brian and said, "Listen son, I am not having two gangs in here, and trying to appease one or the other is not something I am prepared to do.

"I come into my work to enjoy it and if there is any friction, then that takes all the peace away. You were here first son, and doing a great job, so if you are in agreement for Mart to stay, then I need to see a bit of harmony. You don't need to be hugging one another but I insist on a good working relationship. On the other hand, if you feel you cannot do that then I will close his placement and we continue as we are, no one is any worse off."

Brian stood for a second and then said, "If he is prepared to go along with that, then so am I."

Breakthrough

I went back to Mart and explained that I had given Brian the choice of them working together on the understanding that harmony would not be broken for any reason whatsoever.

"Does the big man agree to that?" was Mart's response, now knowing that a quick return to Barlinnie was very much the front runner. "Aye, he did," I said, "so it's something you both can work at if you agree, but Brian is staying here, one way or the other."

He knew the option was against him and I knew it was against his grain to agree, so when he said, "Okay, let's do this," I was as shocked as I was pleased.

This was a big stand down for an old acquaintance to take a back seat as peace was brokered.

Now let me just say that the several months that Mart was with us, he did not break that commitment and on a couple of occasions I heard both men offering each other to make their teas and coffees, so it was a genuine truce that lasted until both of them moved on.

Brian went on to a good job, got a partner and then had a child.

Mart, who was a great worker too, helped to complete our car park and outside pavement to a professional level. On his last day Mart had come into the office when a large truck from Glasgow City Council pulled up (I had contacted our local councillor to ask him to help us with this pavement, not knowing Mart's day of leaving) and put down tarmac on Mart's prepared pavement.

I take my son Barclay to the factory on a weekly basis and he just loves working with the men/women but Mart seemed to drop his guard when Barclay was there. I used to look out of my office window on to the car park and I could not tell who had Downs, Barclay or Mart, as they were so close when they worked away as a team.

I think the biggest change for Mart was the kindness of Walter Souter. Mart's mum had been in hospital and I went to visit her there and then in her home. I noticed that she was a wee mammy that loved holy pictures. I had said this to Walter just as a conversation piece, when he brought in a large embroidery of St John of the Cross by Salvador Dali that was done by an inmate of Peterhead HMP many years prior. He told me to drop it off to Mart's mum as a gift, which I did. Mart came in the following day quite upset.

I was then summoned to my own office to be quizzed about this masterpiece that had been delivered to his mum's house.

"What's this embroidery thing all about Pat?" he inquired.

"O for goodness sake calm down," I said laughing, "I told Walter that your mum had been ill and that when I went to visit her at home she had a number of large Christian pictures on her wall. Walter being Walter decided to give your mum an embroidery that he had had for years. What's the matter with that? It's called compassion Mart."

He stood for a few seconds and then came out with, "Aye, but what is he after?" Mart could just not get it into his head that he was cared for, but if you read his final farewell letter to *Open Gates* he explains it perfectly.

Mart's letter

March 2013

I'm thankful that Open Gates gave me the opportunity for a placement; as I was finding it difficult to find a placement due to being a high profile prisoner.

When I arrived I did not know what to expect, being a fifty-two-year-old man who had never worked. It was a totally different world having to work and being surrounded with people that were not criminals. It did take me a few weeks to settle but once I began I took an interest in the work I was allocated.

The workers at Open Gates supported and helped me to find a new mind-set in the work I was given. For the first time in my life I had job satisfaction and an outlook outside the criminal fraternity.

I took on the task of ground maintenance and this took me out of criminal conversations. Now that I am moving on to open prison I will be back to volunteer with this charity. I have been pleased to see that on my last day at Open Gates the work I started several months ago has been appreciated. Only today, the damaged pavement around the factory I have been repairing was completed by Glasgow District Council when they laid tarmac on my prepared work.

I now feel confident to do manual and semi-skilled work and feel this placement has given me a new outlook.

I would like to thank Open Gates for their support and kindness towards me.

Mart

The past catches up with Mart and BJ

Often I get a chance to talk to a few of our service users privately. They approach me outwith there being anyone around. They are genuinely interested in how I had changed my life around which allowed made me to take the path I am now on.

Mart was one of these men and so was BJ who was interested in my past. Both of these men were murdered not long after they left our supervision. Each man was influenced with my testimony but not enough to change them from their lifestyle.

As for Mart, his past caught up with him when he disappeared suddenly. I got a call from the CID who came to the factory to ask if I had heard anything from him. Apparently he had missed one of his appointments with his care officer which was not allowed as he was out on licence.

As I sat with the two plain clothed officers I assured them that he had not been in touch with me. I also expressed my fears that we maybe had seen the last of Mart. I explained that he did not have enough money to abscond and that the only way he would

260

have missed a compulsory meeting with his parole officer meant that he had been abducted. They were a bit surprised at my fears but these fears were confirmed in December 2015 when Mart's dismembered body was found in undergrowth. His past had caught up with him when he was shot in the head.

As for BJ, he was the very opposite to Mart, being the likeable rogue with a personality that made you laugh, constantly. He was the Del Boy of Possil. Yet this young lad had spent expensive regular months on holiday in Thailand.

My last conversation with him was personal and intense as I advised him to leave the area he was brought up in and go back to Thailand to set up the legal business he was keen on doing.

With a smile he told me that was his intentions. That's the last time I spoke with him before he was caught up in an altercation with a rival gang that attacked and stabbed him. He too died, only because he could not walk away from the lifestyle of addiction he was in.

The heart ache that such lives bring is one of the reasons I love the work I do. I know there is an answer and to get the offender to change is not only beneficial to the offender himself but also to their victims and to both sets of families. One offence causes a trail of heartache and sorrow.

New man – Danny

Danny joined our board over five years ago and I am sure our board will agree that he brings a calmness and a wisdom to our table. He has a way with comforting words that suits his desire and interest in his field to become a top occupational hypnotherapist.

On that first day when we had a meeting in the church office and he was looking around a room full of believers, he said, "I am interested in joining the board but you need to know that I do not believe what you believe."

He went on to say that he would give it a try for one year and we were delighted to have him as our first atheist as a board member – and now Chairman. He is a great asset to our board as all members, I'm sure, would agree, but being a Christian I have made a pact with him. At each board meeting he can open in prayer and I will hypnotise the board!

The vision: onward and upward

With the team we had and now have in place work progressed on the building as we constantly improved it, and now it boasts of a wee premises called *The Café Walt* and a conference room called *The Souter Suite* both in memory of our dear friend Walter.

We have also replaced and upgraded the existing electrical fittings and installed LED lighting in our suspended ceilings.

This is some of the work that we have completed and are involved with:

- Paint Room
- Restoration work area
- IT room
- Furniture show room
- Granny Grove (old furniture)
- Furniture stock and storage
- Research room
- Electrical Goods Room

Add to this well over two hundred men/women who have been NTE/CPO/Volunteers.

We have had groups from:

- NHS Mental Health
- Through Care
- School placements

There are more agencies we use but every one of these folk, no matter how small or how big, have made all this possible without exception.

Then we have our board, our volunteers and workers who believe in what we do. It's the best work I have been involved in and as we grow I see the vision I got over twenty years ago coming into fruition.

On another note *Open Gates* paid for a well to be sunk at an orphanage in Zimbabwe. It was completed and became operational in March 2019. Our Chairman, Danny, had the privilege to witness the first water to come up from the deep. We hope to put a purification plant in to India as soon as it is financially viable.

Epilogue

A few years back while standing in our new *Souter Suite* conference room at the factory, I could see through the trees and onto the window of the Possil Church where I declared my Word from the Lord. I do not have any egg on my face any more – God was faithful in bringing about His vision and keeping His word.

So why the big story? Am I looking for money? What's the catch? These are three questions that would come to mind if I was reading the above tale but I feel that when you read this story you will see how wonderfully our Lord works.

Yes, we do need money for renovations and to run things, but there is a bigger picture here outwith the factory and its vision. It's the people and the lives who have been and are being touched and changed by *Open Gates* and what God is doing.

In the bible Habakkuk 2:2-3 talks about how a vision may tarry but it will be fulfilled in its time. As a Christian I believe that, and I have had the experience of it happening in my life with my son Barclay. So I have history and experience of the Lord moving.

I thank God for my life and the path I have taken, for it has been a path that He has allowed me to go that I might produce fruit that will last, only in His name.

In my elder years I find that family are so precious and so dear. Each one from Tracy to Harris and all in between give me deep joy and contentment. With the blessing of Barclay's birth I think my family will agree that he takes family love on to another plain. I still find that love for my siblings from Helen to Gra-hame and the only regret is the years I missed with them during my apprenticeship in stupidity and impulse.

So can I say that the thrust of this wee story (without becoming super spiritual) is to encourage you to see your vision through no matter how long it takes?

As you can see in Habakkuk, it will happen, it won't be late.

To Him be the Glory.

God Bless.

Pat

Myself with my granddaughter, Riley, and Barclay

Four male generations: myself with Barclay, grandson Dylan and great-grandson Harris

Myself with Barclay and Brogan

Contact Details

For more information on *Open Gates* go to:

https://www.opengates.scot

Open Gates will support prisoners and ex-prisoners through an employment and training programme with the aim of reducing re-offending and stopping the revolving door back into prison. Individuals who have managed to break the cycle will use their experience to mentor and support other offenders to do the same. Operating as a social enterprise, the organisation will manufacture, recycle, and upcycle furniture and white goods and sell to the general public.

7 Dawson Place
Glasgow
G4 9SS
Charity Number: No *SCO 42240*
Mobile: 07400 825 857

Postscript

This book is aimed at offenders who are caught in the never ending circle of crime. It highlights the war of a corrupt nature "self" and of "spirit." So often, good intentions dilute the poor actions we make and take. This war goes on in everyone and not just the offender.

The Apostle Paul writes in Romans 7:14-25 (God's Word):

I know that God's standards are spiritual, but I have a corrupt nature, sold as a slave to sin. I don't realise what I am doing. I don't do what I want to do. Instead, I do what I hate.

I don't do what I want to do, but I agree that God's standards are good.

So I am no longer the one who is doing the things I hate, but sin that lives in me is doing them.

I know that nothing good lives in me, nothing good lives in my corrupt nature.

Although I have the desire to do what is right, I don't do it.

I don't do the good I want to do.

Instead, I do the evil that I don't want to do.

Now, when I do what I don't want to do, I am no longer the one who is doing it. Sin that lives in me is doing it.

So I have discovered this truth: Evil is present with me even when I want to do what God's standards say is good.

I take pleasure in God's standards in my inner being. However, I see a different standard (at work) throughout my body.

It is at war with the standards my mind sets and tries to take me captive to sin's standards which still exist throughout my body.

What a miserable person I am!

Who will rescue me from my dying body?

I thank God that our Lord Jesus Christ rescues me!

So I am obedient to God's standards with my mind, but I am obedient to sin's standard with my corrupt nature.

Prayer

If you have been moved and inspired by this story and the changes that happened in Pat's life through his encounter with Jesus Christ, here is a prayer that will help you on that journey,

Lord Jesus Christ,

I know that I have sinned in my thoughts, words and actions.
There are many good things I have not done and many sinful things I have done.
I am sorry for my sins and now turn from everything I know to be wrong.
I put my trust in You and ask You to forgive me because You gave Your life for me upon the cross.
Gratefully I give my life back to You and ask You to come into my life.
Come as my Saviour to cleanse and forgive me.
Come as my Lord to control me.
Come as my Friend to be with me.
And I will serve you all the remaining years of my life.

Amen.

Appendix 1

Anti-drugs campaigner blasts Government's methadone programme as "bordering on criminal"

One of Scotland's leading anti-drugs campaigners says the Government's methadone programme is "bordering on criminal".

Maxie Richards runs a foundation for recovering addicts and has opposed use of the heroin substitute for more than 20 years.

She said, "You don't treat a drug addict by giving them more drugs.

"When I researched the drug, my fears were confirmed. I think it is bordering on criminal that the Government have been giving it out to people on a huge scale for so long. This is a drug that kills, yet the NHS are giving it to very vulnerable, ill people who come to them for help.

"It was always clear to me that a lot of people were going to die if they took methadone. Now we are seeing that happen in ever increasing numbers."

Maxie runs a rehab centre from her home in Bearsden, near Glasgow. She also runs a home for recovered addicts in remote Tighnabruaich, Argyll.

The 75-year-old mum-of-three added, "The key to helping people recover is to make them feel valued. There isn't a magic spell, you just have to make people feel like they are wanted and have a life worth living.

"At the moment you have a strategy called the Road To Recovery that accepts methadone as a big part of the solution to drug addiction. To me it represents a hopeless road, a road to nowhere.

"I fully support the *Daily Record*'s campaign to have the Scottish Government review the methadone programme.

"I think it is such a waste to let young people spend years on methadone because we don't think there's any hope for them."

Article by John Ferguson: August 27, 2012

Appendix 2

It helped save lives at Dunkirk. Now *Resolute* is saving addicts – newspaper report from *The Herald* at the time.

Former drug users will help in three-year project to restore 1920s Cutter

It arrived in pieces, a shadow of its former self but ready to embark on a long process of rebuilding. It was ravaged and broken, but if it wanted a second chance The Resolute had come to the right place.

The boat landed at the Maxie Richards Foundation in Port Glasgow, where hundreds of former drug addicts have turned their lives around and learned new skills such as carpentry, joinery and upholstery. Bringing The Resolute back to life will be their next major project, and perhaps one of the most special.

The boat, built for cockle dredging on the muddy flats of the Thames, took its place in history after being used in the dramatic rescue of thousands of troops from the beaches of Dunkirk in 1940, when ordinary fishermen came under gunfire as they pulled the soldiers from French soil.

Yesterday, the *Resolute* lay in bits on the floor of the foundation's warehouse. Around a third of the 32ft vessel remains semi-intact, the rest just a collection of ropes, portholes and planks which once made up the fine boat.

As Ms Richards – who is in her early seventies and has worked with addicts for more than 20 years – surveyed the arrival, she said, "That's the state the boys are in when they come here, but we manage to resuscitate them. The boat was going to disappear if someone didn't ask us to help.

"We don't give up on anyone and we didn't want to give up on this boat. It represents so much courage of the men, ordinary men, who sailed her on the channel and took part in the historic rescue."

The *Resolute*, a Bawley Cutter built in 1927, fished throughout the war to help deliver crucial food.

Owner and skipper Eric Osborne returned with a haul one night in May 1940 to be told that the Navy at Southend, just a mile or two down river, wanted the *Resolute* and its fellow fleet ready to travel to Dunkirk at 8am the next day.

The boat was considered a perfect vessel to help collect the soldiers as its flat bottom, which had allowed it to shore up the shellfish at low tide in Essex, meant that it could get close to the beaches and transfer the soldiers to the trawlers which waited in deeper waters.

The story captivated Professor John Atkinson, a health specialist at the University of the West of Scotland, who has a keen interest in the history of boats and links to the Association of Dunkirk Little Ships.

Mr Atkinson was asked if he would be interested in seeing the *Resolute* rebuilt, and three years ago he contacted BAE at its Scotstoun yard to see if the company would be interested in the project.

Naval architects at the firm sourced line drawings and a dossier of information on the *Resolute*, and the original engine has now been faithfully restored by specialists at BAE.

Mr Atkinson then contacted Maxie Richards to see if the foundation was interested in taking part in the restoration.

He said, "The boat has suffered quite a lot of damage over time and there is quite a lot missing of her but I am absolutely delighted that this is happening, and that it will be rebuilt here.

"Meeting up with Maxie on this has been brilliant. This boat helped to save all those people in the past, and now Maxie and these young people will help to save it."

The boat will take three years to completely restore, and it is hoped to move the Resolute to the foundation's residence in Tighnabruaich, Argyll, in time.

Chris Kelly, has trained with the foundation for a year and-a-half, and will work on the project. He said, "One day I would like to think we could see it on the water again. That would be something else."

The Herald January 2008

Other books by Pat Clark

Where the Rubber Meets the Road A Christian book for unbelievers. Published by *Garth* and printed in 2000

A new book by Pat Clark coming soon...

The Inner Sanctuary of the Father's Heart

The Trinity

Acclamation-Agreement-Action

The expanse of the universe was dark, null and void but in El Shaddai's conceived thoughts everything existed. Selection and purpose were in place as the Son stood in agreement with the Father's plan. For the free will of the children of God would come at a great cost.

The inner sanctuary and harbour of the Creator's heart was pregnant with life as He moulded and shaped the children He so much desired. It would be a place that could not be remembered or recognised by those who would be tainted, but in the fullness of time all would know and acknowledge that it was home; the place where every man and woman was conceived.

With eyes that didn't blink, Father looked into the same eyes of His Son and said with lips that barely moved, "My beloved Son, in whom I am well pleased, the time has come for your sacrifice to be agreed on for the birth of man". An agreeing smile of unity and oneness broke on the Son's face. "Let Your will be done," came a reply that echoed throughout eternity.

The emanation of Wisdom looked on, as she witnessed the Trinity's complete and perfect plan for the eternal family. She smiled in delight as she foresaw the final outcome, for she too was part of the home coming of man.

Then the Spirit of the Trinity moved to hover over the formless and empty earth and the darkness that covered the deep water.

Then God said, "Let there be light," and there was light. And the light was good.